SIMPLE STEPS TO

CHANGE

YOUR BUSINESS

YOUR LIFE

Jay A. Livingston, MA

Master Coach

Management Consultant

PracticeSimpleSteps.com

Second Edition

Copyright © 2018 Jay A. Livingston
ISBN-13: 978-1513638577
ISBN-10: 1513638572

Library of Congress Control Number: 2018908612
For information
Author@PracticeSimpleSteps.com

Presented by Bates Hall
Published by CreateSpace

For Szifra Birke

My Coach and Wife

Table of Contents

Enjoy the Ride

I've scheduled the time. The weather is good. But instead of getting dressed and going for a bicycle ride, I'm leaning on the counter in my kitchen, thinking. A week ago I planned this ride, so why am I leaning here redeciding?

I have plenty of time. I told my wife I was going for a ride. And yet here I am making a decision like it's a new idea. This is not the time to redecide my plan. I know better than this—to let my emotions hijack a previous decision. Is inertia an emotion, or an anti-emotion? It's clear that I'm buffeted by short-term impulses and convoluted thinking. That's never a good time to rethink a decision.

Why am I stuck in inaction? There's nothing else I have to do. I was motivated earlier when I planned this ride. I knew what I wanted to do—ride to Westford and back at a moderate pace at a high pedal-spin rate. I'm just not initiating the plan. The mental doohickey that transforms "being" into "doing" seems stuck on idle. I'm standing here frozen in a Parkinsonian-like inertia—I need a nudge to move.

I have long-range goals, all of which would benefit from a ride today. I want to log a total of 2,000 miles on my road bike this year. I know my brain functions best on regular shots of the growth hormones, which I get from exercise. I want to build additional stamina into my aerobic endurance. I want to push further away the inevitable time when age diminishes my abilities. All these are goals that I personally find important and motivating—usually.

But apparently facts, good intentions or goals aren't enough. I'm encased in a soft pudding of inertia. I can get into this kind of mind-mush when I have to push against lethargy or establish a new routine. I was sick and didn't ride for two weeks. My riding routine is disrupted. Not riding took very little brain effort. Now, the small decisions and conscious actions needed to reestablish my routine are draining my willpower reserves quickly. I want to eat. I want to sit. I want to read. I don't want to *do* anything.

In order to establish forward momentum, I need to come up with a step that takes minimal effort but initiates sustained activity. The simplest step I can think of is to pump my bike tires. Fine! I'll just go to the garage and do that.

Now that I'm at the bike, I might as well take my water bottles inside and fill them. I'm moving. The small steps are working. It's easy to keep going. I head to the bedroom to dress in my riding gear. No thinking necessary, just next action followed by next action.

This is what I teach my clients to do when they're bogged down. Just act! Stand up. Take a step. Walk around. Research something. Talk to someone. Just *do* something! Any action toward your goal creates momentum and momentum nurtures motivation. I needed to take a next step. I needed to move just a step or two into action. And then I needed to pay attention to what happened when I acted, what it felt like, what I learned for next time.

That morning I kept moving and rode about thirty miles in two hours on the bike. I morphed from a slug to an athlete. When I returned home and dismounted in the driveway, my inertia had been replaced by a glow of satisfaction. I love being on the road on my bike. I love the sensation of my quads driving a fine piece of equipment up a significant hill. The quiet whir of bike tires on smooth pavement resets my distress level to zero.

The accumulated miles, the exercised-induced growth hormones, the increased aerobic capacity and the slowing of age-related decline for another day are all things I savor after a ride. But the motivation that keeps the pedals spinning is the actual experience of riding.

Developing a new habit—changing—is simple but still involves effort. The process is full of waves of resistance and energy, but as straightforward as taking a next-action step. Development of a new habit is as concrete as digging a ditch and as difficult as redirecting the flow of a river. A new behavior is built pedal stroke by pedal stroke, next action by next action. Initially each push is uphill. The payoff is delayed. Until after a hundred strokes the terrain begins to drop away and you begin to freewheel faster and faster with no effort.

Enjoy the ride!

Why Read This?

If you're trying to be a more organized and effective leader, manager, parent or life partner, this book shows you how to become the person you want to be. To do that you need to practice simple steps.

There Are Practical Ways to Make Change Easier

Even if you've failed many times before, you can learn to make and stick with changes. This time you can change! If, however, you're looking for an approach that promises results with no work, I regret to inform you there are very few of those.

While change isn't rocket science, it does involve neuroscience. Research in this area—sources are noted in the bibliography—points at how to work with your natural tendency to change and to make changing easier. Because our brains manage change and habits in predictable ways, you can learn techniques that take advantage of your biological tendencies and make the process of change easier.

The ideas here will increase the odds you'll change and that the change will be easier and more permanent than changes you've tried to make in the past. The concepts and tools are simple, easy to understand, proven by experience and based on current research.

I'm not going to quote the research—if you're interested, the list of books at the end will help you find the original research. Research is a look at the general tendencies of a group of people, usually college students because they're easy for researchers to find. Research can give each of us a hint about how we may be affected by personal and social circumstances. But we need to explore and see what works best for us. I encourage you to try the suggestions I lay out and see if they work as well for you as they have for me and many of my clients.

Do You Like Overviews?

If you like to know the theoretical background about why we have mixed feelings about change, why we resist it or why we can't stick with a change we really do want to make, the first few sections will give you that view. Understanding why can help motivate, orient and guide you when you find yourself stuck or falling off the change wagon.

Do You Like to Just Jump In?

If you just want quick basic ideas—to just get started—you can always come back later for the overview. Practical ideas form the basis of most sections. But it's easier to change if you understand exactly what you want, what might stand in your way and how you can make the process easier and more effective. I encourage you to take the time to learn the basics underlying change. If you do, you'll probably find it easier to stay on track.

You Can Certainly Change By Yourself

But, for many people, the change process will be even more effective with the support of a group or a professional. If you decide to do that, be sure you look for support that points forward and moves you ahead—too much replaying of past troubles is usually counterproductive. And look for a person or group that uses an approach based on proven techniques not just common societal dogma.

You Can Change!

Change is possible. You've changed many times in the past. Now you need to harness the power of proven approaches to change what you decide, when you decide and then to stick with the new habit.

Consider what you'd like to do differently in your life. Get ready to begin new activities. Start doing things to build new habits. Stick to new behaviors until they're your new default settings.

Changing a Business Means Changing Your Team

Businesses are complex interactions of people—employees and managers, customers/clients/patients and staff, frontline people and potential clients. Learn to change people and all sorts of equations change—client satisfaction, perception of quality, management's investment of time in problem-team members and more.

What I can tell you is that changing yourself will have a profound impact on the people you work with. Understanding how to change yourself will allow you to influence changes in your team. If you work for someone else, you can use the methods of change to influence the person you work for.

Section 1: Getting Started

No matter how many times you've tried to change, no matter how many times you've attempted and failed to get or to maintain the results you wanted, change is possible. Really!

It isn't that change is just theoretically possible. And I don't mean simply that people can change—I mean specifically *you* can change. This isn't some airy affirmation. Change occurs every day in countless places and situations. Can you think of a reason why you're so different that you can't join the parade?

You already change regularly. You learn and adapt, you build new skills, and you adjust to new technology. You change all the time. Now you need to consciously decide to take charge of changes. Change in the way you want.

You can modify tough, long-standing negative habits. You can establish new positive behaviors. This includes the way you relate to colleagues and employees, family and friends. You can improve your reactions and interactions.

I'm not overlooking the fact you've probably tried in the past to change and failed to accomplish what you wanted. I'm not ignoring that you've tried many times to establish a new habit only to slide backward when your attention switched to other important issues in your life. The fact you've failed in the past to institute or maintain a change you desired doesn't preclude that a new effort will be successful—past failures don't predict future failures. In fact, prior attempts tend to increase the odds of future success. The research on quitting smoking reflects this, the more times people have tried to quit the better the odds the next time will stick.

Changing isn't complicated or involved. But for change to take hold, it must feel personally important or interesting. If you're changing for reasons that are essential to you, the odds of success dramatically improve. There are solid techniques to help you deal with inertia, with forgetting to remember what you want to be doing or with conflicting feelings. But not much will work if you're just trying to change because someone else says you should.

Change can be exciting. It's an ongoing opportunity to remake yourself. We're never fixed personalities or done learning. We'll always be works in progress.

Research shows that you're probably pretty good at knowing how much you've changed in the past, and pretty bad at guessing how much you'll change in the future. So be skeptical about strong feelings that you only have a limited ability to change. Many people like you have changed as they grew older, had more experience and faced new challenges.

Predictability and Stability are Temporary Options

Change might grow quietly or noisily, but it will eventually roll over us. We can invest our energy in futile attempts to hold it back. We can refuse to willingly adopt new habits that will allow us to fully participate in our constantly changing world, or we can work to get out ahead of the inevitable new wave that will revitalize our old world.

If you feel any doubt that change will come, remember at the most fundamental level our bodies change relentlessly. Bob Dylan sang, "He not being born is busy dying." Every cell in your body renews itself many times in your life. In a similar way, every day and every experience you have changes your operating system—personality and habits. The odds are you're really different from the person you were ten or twenty years ago.

Change will continually happen, with or without your permission, not just at times you initiate it because a situation demands it. You can fight change or embrace it—it makes little difference to the tide of change. Ride it or drown in it—the wave of change will sweep onward.

Since you're reading *Simple Steps to Change*, it seems safe to assume you're ready to try to nudge the inevitable changes toward outcomes you might like.

We're Ambivalent About Change

Most of us have certain areas of our lives we'd like to change, but we only want to change to the point where our vision or goal of a better world or better "us" is achieved. This process of hoping or trying to make the world or ourselves better—toward what we imagine is a superior way—comes to a stop when growing feelings of instability make us uncomfortable.

This process is clearly played out in social change. For a society to work, we need people who try to keep things stable, to conserve the habits and patterns of the past. But too much stability will eventually lead to a risk of social decline from a lack of new ideas and passion for life. Ideas and energy come from unmet needs and unaccomplished goals.

For a society to be resilient, it needs encouragement from "progressives" to strive for new goals and caution from "conservators" to not throw away too easily the hard-won order. This spectrum of "Go slow" and "Let's try something a little different" tends to balance out to create significant resilience even in the face of inevitable changes we don't choose.

As individuals we face the same conflicting pulls. We want to change, and we feel an emotional drag to preserve current habits. Old habits—positive and negative—take less energy. The inertia of an established habit is powerful.

Yet the prospect of a new and improved us is also powerful. What greater quest is there than to be able to recreate ourselves as the person we would like to be? The idea of an easier path through our work and relationships, of more satisfaction and less frustration is truly motivating.

Positive, Clear Thinking Can Help Control Emotions

To overcome inhibiting emotions like lethargy, anxiety or doubt, which we may be barely aware we're affected by, takes deliberate thinking. We can think—use our brain's prefrontal cortex—to constrain our emotional reactions, which are powered by our amygdala. With practice we can act more on the desired outcomes we've thought through rather than on our old, impulsive, reactive responses. We can act more on our true needs and not just easy habits, more on our long-term goals and less on immediate gratification.

Thinking clear thoughts about concrete facts helps to challenge hot emotions and persuasive emotional pulls. This process is similar to flinching, realizing it was only a shadow that passed over you and then relaxing. Your flinches—automatic reactions—can be modified by confirming danger isn't imminent and then trying to identify the facts you should be considering.

In a stressful situation, naming your feelings is one way to bring your thinking into the process. For example,

> *I recognize I'm acting unprofessionally. I'm feeling frustrated. What is a specific thing I could do to stop this emotional slide? I'll stop talking and take a moment to identify what might be frustrating me.*

> *Oh, I feel challenged. It feels like they aren't respecting my experience or intelligence. How can I stay with my best thinking? I'll strategize about how to welcome their critique while reminding myself I don't need to prove anything to them right now.*

Recognizing and being able to name the emotions that get in your way, that hijack your navigation systems, moves a roadblock slightly to one side. If you leave these emotions unexamined, they can throw up resistance to change or drag at your attention or energy. You'd do better to invest in the new habit. (We'll look at this more in the sections on "Keep Your resistance in Check" and "Temper Your Emotional Reactions.")

Your Thinking Will Affect Your Attitude and Energy

Having a personal philosophy or attitude that welcomes change will promote an openness to it. A philosophy acts as an anchor to ground you to the larger reality you're trying to create. Thoughts you repeat to yourself are likely to jump into your head when you're stressed. An attitude that welcomes continual adjustments and change in your approach to life is a good way to encourage yourself to develop a life-long habit of easier change.

Our brains prefer to invest as little energy in our day-to-day activities as possible. We form habits in order to make fewer decisions and use less energy. If you develop the habit of welcoming change, you'll expend less effort bemoaning the effort it takes to change.

You certainly don't have to welcome all changes. The changes incurred from a broken leg or dismissal from a job are hard to appreciate. But if you welcome the fact of change, you'll spend less time lamenting your fate and instead start the process of making changes needed to adapt to your situation and move on toward a more interesting place in life.

In complex systems—think of people, organizations and societies, anything with more than a few variables—any change will likely have unintended results—some good, some upsetting but unforeseeable. Email brought spam and cars brought more deadly accidents. Each change we appreciate—i.e., cheaper clothes and food—is embedded in a system where the occurrence of any particular change will also change things we don't necessarily want altered—such as wages or social upheaval.

Until we accept the complexity of change—and of resisting change—we may feel like victims of unusual circumstances. Change is just the process of life, which we have to deal with as long as we're alive—death does appear to create stability in our thought processes, if not our physical condition.

Teach your children to plan for and manage change in their lives and you've given them a more valuable tool than any static political, religious or economic theory. They will spend more of their time affecting changes that lead toward the world they would like to see and less railing against fate. Teach your employees to seek growth and expect, and look, for productive changes and you create the foundation of a learning organization.

Make Change Successful Instead of Stressful

I hope the tools presented here will help you create a life and workplace that are ready for the changes that will come at you, and that these tools will prepare you to utilize those changes to your advantage. Create an environment where people are continually encouraged to grow professionally as well as personally, and you'll have employees who can react thoughtfully and take much of the burden of change and surprise off your shoulders. Decide that you'll try to find a way to thrive in the face of a changing world, professional practice or business approach, and you'll generally find yourself creating value while others are still frozen in confusion or nursing their disgruntled feelings.

Stop hiding from or ignoring the changes taking place in your relationships, private and professional, and you'll discover more comfort, less stress and possibilities that might reduce the work of incessantly trying to smooth out miscommunications.

I'll say a bit more about the inevitability of change in the first section. But the beginning of making change successful instead of stressful is to simply stop fighting it and learn the "secrets" of more natural change.

What Else is In Here?

Section two will look at how you can train yourself to have a better attitude toward change. It's easy, particularly as you get older, to resist changes. We become comfortable with how things are and have developed habits to deal with things as we know them—we're hungry, we eat, then suddenly we gain a bit of weight but we're comfortable eating, so we continue and resist cutting back.

Instead of focusing on how unfair it was that I couldn't eat all the snacks and desserts I wanted, I made some major changes in my diet by reminding myself again and again, when I was tempted by low-nutrition, high-calorie food, that what I was craving wasn't "food." It was entertainment, emotionally comforting, good tasting, but not "food" in the best sense of that word. It was easier to welcome change as cleaning up the junk-food contents of my plate instead of reducing my intake.

If you practice convincing yourself that change is a normal state of affairs, which of course it is, it's easier to change old habits—they're only temporary ways you did things. You aren't fixed and locked, you're flexible and open to new ideas.

Section three offers some questions to help sort through the myriad of change opportunities that clamor for attention on a day-to-day basis. Thinking about these types of questions will aid you in choosing which changes you may want to actively pursue and which to sidestep if you can.

Change is inevitable, yet there are also stupid ideas that need to be ignored. But ideas that you should discard as unrealistic—too far ahead of their time to be practical or just plain ignorant—may have some aspects that are potentially valuable. Recognizing those aspects and not discarding them with the rest of the idea is the challenge for thought leaders and groundbreakers. Change is a complex process that often occurs because small ideas are scavenged from more complex possibilities to create unexpected approaches.

Finding valuable directions to pursue and the tools to implement change is an ongoing challenge. But the next sections are full of practical techniques to help make the process easier.

Section four explains how to develop one of the fundamental aspects of success in life and change—self-discipline. Self-discipline, willpower or self-control isn't just something you're born with. It can be developed and it makes change much more manageable. Research shows children who are taught self-control do better as adults. And don't despair. Self-discipline can be learned as an adult.

By using the ideas in section four, you can help your kids achieve a brighter future, increase the resilience of your employees and kick your and your business's success to the next level. With a better-developed ability to manage yourself, you'll find change easier to implement.

While each change you make is different, if you pay attention to the processes you use, you'll quickly begin to recognize some fundamental techniques that are helpful in most situations. Section five outlines some of these basics. If you'd like to go directly to an action you can try, before you commit to reading the entire book, you might jump to section five. These hints aren't the whole story, but each one has value that can be applied in a variety of situations. Of course, I'd be remiss if I didn't tell you that their value is most often enhanced when they're built into a series of steps that reinforce each other.

There are times when each of us wishes we could change without much effort. The ideas in section six offer some hope for that. These are things you can do to set up your environment so you might change habits without thinking about them. You'll learn specific ideas, based on the best research, for making successful changes with minimal effort. They work. Research proves it.

Section seven gives you some weapons to use against the terrible demon of resistance. Resistance is a guerrilla fighter—it uses indigenous forces against you. Knowing where those forces get their supplies and what their weaknesses are can reduce their effectiveness. Resistance is often fighting to protect us from concerns that are old and perhaps irrelevant. We need to be clear which of these old anxieties are still legitimately of interest to us and which need to be retired.

It's easy to assume that the ways we react to stress and frustration are basically fixed. But as client after client of mine can attest, irritation, anxiety, frustration and many other negative emotional reactions can be changed. Hope, joy and appreciation can be developed. Section eight focuses on how to become more effective at regulating—changing—your emotional reactions. Even small successes in this area can make your life and work a lot more relaxed.

Section nine is devoted to using lists to help facilitate change. People who want to increase their follow-through on commitments and increase productivity at work will find this section a great place to read or scan for quick ideas and some notions to play with.

Section ten encourages you to refine the systems you use at work to manage your responsibilities—projects, tasks, organization and time management.

Change is a broad concept, which is helpful to understand in its totality. There are many specific types of change. Changing your thinking is different from changing your emotional reactions. Changing your daily health habits requires different tweaks than starting a significant new project or setting and achieving an ambitious goal in an area that you've previously been pretty casual about. Sections eleven through twenty focus on specific ways to change in widely different areas.

I think it's entirely possible to work by yourself and to change after hearing the information presented here and practicing the simple steps suggested. But I'd be remiss to not note that many people find it easier to work with a group—think Weight Watchers, Toastmasters or professional study groups—or with a coach. In the conclusion I'll give you a bit of information to help choose a group or coach to work with and for you.

Change can be fun once you get a new habit established. It's the transition from the old way to the new way that's difficult. We're forced to walk through the valley of confusion, swim in the pool of uncertainty and face the dragons of doubt. Either you need to find a way to enjoy the adventure or you'll likely suffer through the quest.

When you get to the other side, you'll feel satisfaction knowing you've joined the ranks of those who know they can change when required. This will make it easier to set out on the next learning adventure. The approach to the mountain will be familiar, you'll know what equipment to bring and you'll know that you have the discipline and persistence to face the obstacles.

Section 2: **Change is a Part of Life**

There are few things in your life that are more inevitable than change. The circumstances of your life, your style of living and your physical body will all continually change.

On the other hand, there are few things more difficult than trying to purposely change or adapt to changes in your lifestyle, your habits or the waning of your physical abilities. Change is such a ubiquitous part of our lives that it would seem we'd have had sufficient practice to have developed proficiency, but most of us are still woefully unprepared and unskilled.

History, fiction and our own lives are awash in stories of people who spiral into catastrophe because they can't change their approach to common but difficult situations. These stories involve ordinary people acting like they've always acted in spite of a new circumstance that challenged their established habits. This new challenge was like many they'd faced before, but this time their old response failed them and led to despair, desperation or destruction.

Edgar Schein, professor emeritus at MIT Sloan School of Management, writing about Digital Equipment Corporation's failure, explained that, if a company is successful, its values tend to harden into unspoken assumptions about effective strategies. When the business environment changes, the organization may not adapt. It may reject ideas that don't fit its preconceived notions of a successful strategy.

Even when the consequences aren't of the Greek-tragedy scale, not knowing how to change can get in the way of your goals and aspirations.

> I grew up with parents who "believed" in noncompetition in life and games. At any gathering my dad would organize whoever was there to play volleyball. His aim was to set the ball up at least

four or five times for other players on your team. My dad's games always had lots of participation and no hurt feelings.

But what a disastrous philosophy to bring to sports. I quit football because I got tackled. I boxed until I got hit in the face. I ran track but got confused when I was about to pass a runner in front of me. I couldn't change my approach from non-compete to compete.

I got a glimpse of what I needed to change when I accidently passed someone and took fourth in the state track meet my senior year. It took twenty-two more years before I had built my change abilities and could pass anyone in front of me and feel satisfaction and pride.

The odds are no one explained to you that your life would be easier if you became an expert at changing your habits. Most people, even when they think a change might be good, continue to follow old habits and notions. They don't change even when their habits are persistently ineffective and don't achieve the desired outcome.

Society Values Consistency

It's not just that we've never been actively tutored in the mechanics of change. Cultural wisdom seems to value consistency more than learning from mistakes and changing. There is even a sense that needing to change means you're flawed or inadequate in some way. Not that any enlightened person would say we shouldn't learn, it's just that if you change on a regular basis, you may be suspected of being inconsistent, of flip-flopping, rather than being someone who continues to learn and grow. You probably won't be celebrated as a learner. Calling someone changeable has been more of an insult than calling them unyielding. And yet you need to adapt to new circumstances and information all the time.

My mother was pretty accepting of my decision at twenty-one to not eat meat. She went out of her way to make me a vegetarian Thanksgiving the first year. The second year we ran into some issues.

> I had cut back on fats and my mother was surprised, "I thought you were vegetarian. I didn't know that you'd changed again."

> She wasn't really concerned about what I ate. She was struggling to open up to the idea that my diet was something I might continue to adjust as I learned about health or that my maturing body required fewer calories. She ate close to what her mother ate, and not that differently from how her grandmother ate.

> Now she gets it and at ninety-six is able to adjust the content and quantity of her diet better than most people.

Run a quick thought experiment for yourself. Think of a person. If you see dramatic changes in their thinking and behavior that are at odds with your personal view of the world, would you value the person more or worry about their inconsistency? If I tell you that you can have greater success by changing, do you feel energized by the thought of success or tired at the thought of needing to change? When I tell you that you could avoid ninety percent of all dental problems by flossing every day, do you leap at the chance to take charge of your health or slink away from the thought of a nightly pattern that needs doing whether you're tired, sick or passionately attracted to someone waiting in your bedroom?

Old Habits Let Us Relax

We develop patterns of behavior—habits—in order to save energy. We can complete most common daily tasks without the need for conscious thought or decisions, both of which take brain energy. It's easiest to just let habits run us down the usual path, in the usual direction.

No wonder we resist change. Although a new habit may eventually help us be more effective in our lives, initially change means extra work. To change we need to keep in mind abstract, far-off, long-term goals and resist the tendency to allow our brain-energy-saving habits to navigate or our short-term impulses to lead us.

> Until new behaviors become old habits they require extra work. I want to lose weight to make it easier to climb hills on my bike. But I get tired just thinking about stopping to consider instead of grabbing a handful of my chocolate-covered espresso beans. I resist change like a fighter at the Alamo, ready to die rather than retreat from sweets.

The Value of a New Habit is Unknown

We can't necessarily know the value of a new habit until we've practiced it and it becomes an unconscious pattern. The new habit may or may not offer a potential reward, and that reward may or may not come to fruition. Even if all works out, how much must we invest in increased focus and energy to reap the reward? To initiate the change process we have to value the potential change. In some cases we need to value just the possibility of learning something about ourselves. Only later will we know whether we've saved enough energy that the effort to build the new habit was worth it.

If we explore even a few of the numerous new behaviors, which we assume might have value, we'll surely try some projects that won't give any appreciable return on our time investment. But we may have new insights, if we're paying attention. The idea of experimentally investing in business opportunities or personnel training opportunities is a solid notion, but we can also evaluate potential changes in our habits on the basis of the value propositions they offer. I'll give you some ideas how to sort through the myriad of change opportunities in the next section.

If you're reading this, you're probably one of the few who want to do more than just wish you could change yourself, your business culture or your employees. You've most likely tried any number of things. You're probably ready to invest in an experiment, or at least hear more about how to make changing easier. But even if you're ready to try, don't be surprised if you feel tired at the thought of resisting your version of chocolate-coffee-bean reduction.

How You Think is How You're Likely to Feel

If lethargy or resistance begin to creep in, I'd suggest you begin the process of change by intentionally nudging your thinking or feelings about change in a more positive direction. Positive thinking makes the whole process easier.

Try moving beyond resistance and even beyond just accepting change as inescapable, to actually embracing change by looking for positive possibilities and feeling good about it. Shift your perspective and you might come to see and feel resistance as the waste of time it is, and change as an interesting learning experiment. You're less likely to squander your energy fighting the inevitable, forward-moving momentum of change.

Thinking about change as a broad topic, and thinking about how you feel about change, are actually important steps toward changing. Our motivation, energy, emotions and success rates are all deeply affected by how and what we think. Think about realistic positive aspects of change and your odds of making headway increase.

> In my twenties, I ruined my intimate relationships by trying to change my partners so that I wouldn't have to change—change made me feel out of control. It seemed so obvious that, if I could get my partners, friends and family to do things my way—what I thought of as the "right way"—the world would be more understandable and I'd be less anxious.
>
> Ah, the arrogance, idealism and pigheadedness of youth.

Of course making the effort to control—stop things from being different, from changing—was one of the most effective ways I could have imagined to spike my anxiety.

When I attempted to let go of my notion that there was a set order, and accepted that I'd have to get comfortable with change and chaos, I had to find someplace to begin.

Sitting alone in a one-room, tarpaper shack in Wyoming, I created a refrain for myself. *The world is chaotic, and my only comfort will be in finding a way to get comfortable with chaos.*

After a few years I modified it. *I want to be better at accepting and riding the wave of chaos than anyone else.* You can see that my non-competitive upbringing had major cracks.

It doesn't work to simply repeat fluffy, unrealistic self-affirmations of the "I love to change" variety. You need forward-looking statements that remind you of the positive benefits, rather than those that bemoan the negatives or past failures. And they have to be believable or you'll likely unconsciously ignore them.

- *This is a new opportunity to learn something.*
- *If I can do this thing this time, it would be really helpful.*
- *There are good aspects to this change.*
- *I've changed before. This is just another step.*
- *Past failures have taught me a lot. Success is more possible this time.*

It's fascinating and wonderful how we can remake our fundamental beliefs about ourselves. Until you've tried it, it's hard to believe how effective it can be. When you repeatedly "correct" your thinking, the corrected notion slowly becomes your new reality. Cognitive reframing— thinking differently, having a new perspective—is change at the most profound level. Thinking differently changes your life view and eventually your neurological structure. All lifestyle habits are built on the framework of thinking and they'll tend to be easier to change, if you've developed a new way—a new habit—of thinking about change.

I regularly speak with my clients about the pervasiveness of change in our lives. I know that if I want to help them accept change, I need to help them reframe their notion that change is a burden thrust on them by other people and outside forces. They need to hear that change is common and natural, and they need to develop expertise in welcoming it. I repeat and repeat the idea over and over until they begin to consider it, and eventually say it to themselves.

In my role as a consultant and coach, I model a way of thinking that embraces change. In my experience, if my clients know there is at least one person in their lives who works at changing every day, they'll experience just a bit of social pressure to adopt a new attitude—change will become more normal. I want to be a reminder of the possibility of embracing a new, personal philosophy of change. And I want to be obvious as someone who works at changing his old, patterned reactions and daily habits through persistent effort.

For many years I worked to change my profound fear and anxiety that was compounded by childhood experiences.

> I was bullied and physically assaulted throughout junior high and high school. The sometimes violent attacks left me with permanent physical scars. But the most debilitating effect was an incessant, fearful awareness of the possibility of aggression and bodily injury. Any confrontation, including sports competition, left me shaking and anxious.

> In young adulthood I made a deliberate choice to change my reactions. I wanted to change from feeling dread and like a potential victim, to understanding hostility as one aspect of life that I didn't have to like, but that no longer froze my thinking.

I took full-contact kickboxing classes, trained and began working as a dog behaviorist specializing in rehabilitating seriously aggressive dogs and studied techniques for managing fear. Every step of the way was uncomfortable and exhausting. But I was determined to understand the process of changing primal reactions. I also had a goal of making an impact by helping others change.

I began to fathom the full scope of my avoidance, not just of aggression, but even competitiveness. It was then that I pushed further into my discomfort zone and took up competitive sailing. (Incidentally, I was also afraid of unexpected incidents around water, which sailing can be full of.) I knew how to persist and was learning to regulate my impulse to avoid anxiety. I used those skills to explore how to heighten motivation, quiet self-critique, persevere in the face of physical exhaustion. As I explained earlier, even winning wasn't easy. I had to push past my fear of being too assertive. I worried that winning would bring ostracism.

I gained insight and internal growth. Equally important was the significant income and satisfaction from successful stints as a dog behaviorist, as a Coast Guard-licensed captain and as a sailing coach.

Currently, I'm exploring changing a fundamental aspect of my personality further through training and participating in endurance bicycle events. I want to see how to manage motivation in the face of perceived exhaustion and discomfort.

The support of a community of sailors and bicyclists has been a major help. These likeminded individuals have often unwittingly given me encouragement to push into my resistance and reluctance.

We're Influenced By What We See Around Us

Research shows we're affected by the attitude and style of our friends and acquaintances and by their friends. Choose your friends wisely! Look for people who model change. Since society invests so little effort in preparing us for change, we each need to go out of our way to seek friends, colleagues, coaches, therapists, teachers or others who are positive about life, who are continually trying to change, trying to reshape their own attitudes—professed and internal—toward personal change.

Another way to think about this is to minimize your exposure to people with a fixed mindset—those who think things are as they are and can't be changed. Each person who embraces change brings a smidgen of social encouragement into our lives. And that social encouragement makes our own process easier.

Tone Down Your Inner Critic

Pay attention to your internal voice. It's common to have a dispiriting personal critic. Many people regularly give themselves anti-pep talks that are full of negatives and discouraging.

> *What I'm doing won't lead to anything exciting.*

> *What's the point? I won't get to the finish line. I never do.*

> *Find a way to avoid doing this. It won't work anyway.*

> *I'm tired.*

> *I always blow this stuff. I can't change.*

The voice is yours. Take charge of it. Demand that it talks to you realistically and with respect for your ability to change. You've practiced the demotivating words and attitude enough that they've become a habit. Like any habit, practice something different and that will become your new habit.

Adjusting the words in your head isn't the result of a change in attitude but usually precedes it—think a certain way and then begin to feel that way. Decide what attitude would be most helpful to you. Teach your inner voice to talk about life in that way.

Change is learning, and I like learning new things.

I'm a person who wants to value change.

I want to be flexible.

Resisting change is an old thought and feeling. A new habit just takes repetitions.

Reframing—changing—your talk and attitude is crucial. We automatically focus on what we're used to focusing on—what society has encouraged and validated us for noticing and caring about. Whatever you've practiced thinking and feeling you will focus on—become aware of.

If you're beginning to see the circular pattern in change, you're getting it. Embracing change makes it easier to change, and if you want to change, it's important to embrace the normality and possibility of change in your thinking. We're slowly walking onto the field of change and getting close to the swamp of resistance where all is possible and where doubts are rampant, where old patterns seem sacred just because they're established and new patterns may sound heretical.

When you're up to your knees in the muck of change, you'd better have a notion that change will lead you to interesting new vistas. Otherwise you will exhaust yourself and turn back to the old paths you've always used.

Ideas to Ponder

- Change is what living organisms do. We need to change constantly in virtually every area of our lives.
- We can fight change, but we will never prevail for long.

- We are born with the ability to change.
- Even if we do nothing, we will be forced to change again and again.
- When we consciously decide to change, our old habits and our brain's pull to save energy will work against us.
- Change involves an ending to how things used to be. Even if you choose to end it, it can feel like a loss.
- We can and do change many things and often.
- How we think about change will affect how we feel about change. And how we feel about change will affect how easily and how well we change.

Accept yourself as a changer and each step after that becomes a bit easier. Perhaps tell yourself, *I'm a changer. I want to be able to look at this situation with new eyes.*

At the elite level of sports, winning is usually about who has the most ability to manage their feelings, who can frame the situation in a positive way and use the most effective perceptions to motivate and focus their efforts. In the game of life, satisfaction and success on your own terms also means managing your feelings and perceptions, and finding the positive aspects of the next new thing.

Section 3: **But Not Just Any Change**

So change may be inevitable, but that doesn't mean all new possibilities are going to be positive or that you should embrace them. Often it makes sense to drag your feet, to keep to the old way for a while longer until you gather more experience or information.

You probably already have a natural resistance to change in certain areas and an eagerness to change in others. The pressure to change a daily health habit—exercise, floss, eat better or less—may raise resistance in you, but the opportunity to change to a newer technology, car or house may sound inviting. Unexamined eagerness and resistance both have drawbacks.

When faced with pressures and opportunities to change, we need a checklist to consult. Here are some questions you might ask yourself before running away, standing your ground or advancing toward a new idea.

What Might Lead Me to Resist or Accept This Change?

Of course you're affected by past influences. Asking this question reminds you to weigh how you're being pushed around by old, out-of-date responses. Your quick, intuitive responses are often full of wisdom, but can also be dangerously biased shortcuts. Your slow, deliberate considerations may focus only on information that confirms your old habits unless you stretch to consider all the possibilities.

Try to get the best answers by listening well to your best intuition and your best thinking. And then use each to keep a check on the other. Start by simply asking questions that will help engage your more deliberate processes, and then pay particular attention to small, quiet doubts.

I've sailed since I was a young adult. For the first twenty years I bought and sailed conservative boats—slower but more stable, those that could realistically handle worse weather than anything I would ever face where I sailed.

My anxiety went up when I considered switching to boats that would be more responsive in the light winds that predominated in my sailing venues. I identified myself as a sailor of stable boats, not fast boats. I knew stable boats and they were my security blanket.

I realized that my penchant for stable boats was a past choice that wasn't necessarily valid given my now extensive level of experience. I thought it through and decided I was ready for a more responsive boat. I began to talk to myself. *Fast is an important part of safety*—true, not a fake affirmation. *An experienced sailor can sail a fast boat safely.*

Now, when I consider entering a race I ask myself, *Are the venue and the conditions appropriate for a fast, nimble boat?* I see myself as an all-around sailor who can adjust to many situations.

Is This in My Interest or Someone Else's?

When you're simply following someone else's dictate, you're less likely to change successfully and less likely to sustain the change. There are often good reasons to follow someone else's encouragement, but until you understand and agree that doing so also meets *your* best needs, slow down.

It may not be easy to tell whether you're resisting because the proposed change isn't your idea, because it sounds too hard or maybe because it feels at odds with your fundamental goals or interests.

A new client asked me to help her change from being a therapist to a coach. I asked why she wanted to make the change. She said she and her husband were researching how to make her practice more successful and he suggested that coaches had more flexibility to serve a wider range of clients.

> When I asked if she liked helping people, she lit up and started talking about the satisfaction she got from seeing people understand the complex influences they were reacting to. She said that when people cried because they understood a new truth about their lives, it made her feel like she had a purpose in life.
>
> She quickly understood that coaching was really her husband's idea and not one where she would likely find the same level of joy and meaning. We changed our coaching focus to think about how she might change her therapy practice to attract additional clients.

Would you invest the same effort if no one else were encouraging or demanding you do it? If you're thinking about trying to change because it will please someone else, then ask if keeping them happy is an important goal for you. Are you simply avoiding a difficult conversation with them? Or are the difficult conversations already happening and you're deciding that this change is in your best interest?

Is This What I Want to Be Doing in Two Years?

You can understand which changes to undertake, if you have an idea what your goals are.

You need to think about the future in order to evaluate an opportunity or project. But be very careful. Don't fool yourself into thinking that you can know what will actually happen. You can't precisely predict the future.

Thinking about what *might* happen is an exercise that keeps you alert to possibilities even when you can't know what *will* happen with any certainty. Thinking about possibilities will tend to help keep you on your toes, nimble, ready to adjust as changes present themselves.

Understanding some of the possible scenarios you might face can also help you not overcommit to a notion you have.

Basketball and football players know the pitfalls that occur when they commit to a defensive move or strategy too early—they get faked out and move opposite to the way their opponent goes. You need to move in a general direction, but hedge a bit so that you can still swing back before it's too late. The best move is to try to place yourself so that you're in a better position to cover two directions until there is a committed play—development—that you can react to with decisive action.

Knowing what goals or long-term interests you're trying to protect will allow you to have a touchstone for evaluating the present pressures to change. Is this change an opportunity or a distraction? Is it best to commit or hesitate?

Does This Distract Me?

Again, this type of question should encourage you to stop and consider. Taking the time to think will tend to interrupt any impulsive or automatic processes. If a change will require a large investment of your time, contemplate what other project you may have to take a step back from—few of us have enough extra time to add a project without moving another one to a lower priority.

Some changes are choices, others aren't. Don't ignore or resist a change that's inevitable, whether you want it or not. Resisting will suck up valuable energy. This is true whether the change is to your profession, your company or your personal life. You want to be alert when a wave of change is about to break, one that will wash away your previous assumptions.

You also want to identify opportunities and adapt before your competition does. There's a huge advantage to recognizing an uncommon opportunity—even if it's strange and uncomfortable as it may seem at first encounter—and then finding some way to benefit from its possibilities.

You need to evaluate new trends and odd ideas for their staying power and for their potential to destroy your old conventions. Discomfort and lack of understanding are not a sufficient basis for rejecting change. History is filled with wrong proclamations from experienced experts—motion pictures with sound were seen as silly; TV couldn't replace radio when it forced you to sit in one place; Japan could only make cheap stuff; you needed to run a business with an authoritarian structure or no one would be productive.

Your tendencies to resist changes and to want things to remain static need to be kept under close watch. Here are a few questions that may help you recognize changes that are probably inevitable, and may eventually displace your current assumptions.

What Basic Need Does This Change Address?

It's often hard to look past the oddness of new ideas and see whether they have the potential for making things better. Try asking questions in a positive way. *How will this work? If this were to work, why would it succeed?*

You want your questions to pull you past easy answers and your initial responses, such as the new idea is too odd to work. You need to dwell in the land of possibility for just a minute. Try to see into the future where peoples' basic needs—for safety, significance, more efficiency, control over their lives—will likely persist. Solutions that address basic needs are likely to remain relevant.

It's also helpful to recognize that aspects of new ideas may be powerful without the entire thing having staying power. The idea of selling Pet Rocks was a brilliant introduction to the power of a story to create emotional connections, although there wasn't much long-term payback in investing in a pile of rocks.

Are Young People Showing Interest in This Idea?

The young—this means those younger than you are today—tend to be willing to try new things. Those new to a field often look at the old issues with an open mind. You ignore trends in youth culture at your own risk.

I'm not just talking about technology trends. Each generation brings its learning and history to the workplace. Millennials—who've heard lots of affirmations from their parents and teachers—came into the workplace expecting that they would be appreciated for small accomplishments. Older managers who fail to adjust to this new attitude aren't retaining the best people on their teams.

Can I Think of a Way I Can Improve on This Idea?

This type of question forces you to think through the specifics of an idea. Imagine you're living in the early 1900s and facing the advent of wireless radio to replace the telegraph. How could you improve on that idea? What other uses might it have that you could promote? Remember, someone eventually came up with a wireless doorbell, a garage-door opener and a remote car starter.

The question encourages you to look at your basic assumptions and think about possibilities not just problems or an idea's strangeness. Questions can help you either see a better way than you're currently pursuing or to recognize a limiting assumption you probably want to investigate further.

Asking yourself or others questions keeps your mind and options open to ideas and helps you resist the natural bias against new mindsets. It's fine to hesitate, but try to do so on the basis of relevant doubts, not because you've forgotten how to question your beliefs.

Hopefully you're becoming more comfortable with the idea that change itself both is and isn't an option, and you're less comfortable with wasting your energy resisting inevitable changes or chasing silly ideas.

As you learn different ways that you can make changes more easily and more permanently, you'll see that trying, and learning from trying, are keys to recognizing and making the most of opportunities.

You'll never recognize all the good changes you might make or all of the ones that will waste your time, but if you develop comfort with self-directing your learning and gain experience approaching new ideas with questions, you'll stay open to possibilities. And that's a good predictor of your ability to institute positive changes.

Section 4: **Self-Discipline Doesn't Have To Be an Olympic Sport**

This is the point where self-discipline insists on getting its due. For most people, this is also where discouragement can start polluting their motivation. Increasing self-discipline sounds like hard work and, if you only look at your history, it may feel like past attempts were mostly followed by failures and therefore not worth it.

Here is some context about the thing we call self-discipline, and then some specific, practical ideas about how to get your self-discipline muscle in better shape.

Building Self-Discipline

Imagine you've been trying off and on for years to increase your strength by lifting two hundred pounds once or twice every few months. If I then told you I had a secret way to increase your strength, which wasn't very hard and was guaranteed to work, you'd probably be extremely skeptical. The secret of course would be to lift lighter weights much more often and build up your capacity. This would be a scientifically-based, achievable path toward strength gains that most people could do.

If you want to develop more discipline, you can. The secret is to build capacity by lifting small discipline efforts more often.

You'll need a small amount of self-control to begin the process, but additional discipline can be developed even for those beginning from a below-average starting point. For the few of you who claim that you have no self-discipline, it's worth noting that it has taken self-discipline just to read or listen this far.

Social Truths That May Get in Your Way

Society has developed some polarized views of self-discipline. People use lots of different words for self-discipline—self-control, self-regulation, willpower, self-management. What we're talking about is the notion of taking responsibility for your actions.

When it comes to taking responsibility, there are coaches and therapists who feel it's unfair to hold certain challenged individuals responsible for fully controlling their emotions or actions.

Social policy and attitudes can easily swing on whether it's productive or not to blame people for addictions or habits that have a strong basis in individual neuro-wiring. Some say it's certainly reasonable to require people to control their impulses and tendencies, that no one should get a "get out of jail free card." Others point out that if biological wiring makes it very difficult for an individual, how can society insist on them doing something they can't do?

I encourage you not to get caught in the extreme dichotomy of that argument. It doesn't reflect the full range of possibilities in the real world. I'll immediately concede that individual neurology makes it harder for some to control impulses or resist temptations. Those individuals are going to have a more difficult time and may well be deserving of some compensatory time to develop a difficult new habit. But of course, having challenging brain wiring doesn't mean that those individuals are allowed to give up trying to develop control.

Individuals with less control over their attention and ability to plan and follow through have a higher possibility of abusing alcohol and drugs. Few of us would suggest abandoning these individuals as incapable of change. We also wouldn't simply forgive or forget if they caused major harm to others because of their genetic difficulties. Something may be more difficult for me than for you, but you at least expect me to work at developing an approach that addresses that weakness.

Research shows that self-control can be developed and strengthened in children and adults. Those with difficulties hope people will understand that they have to work harder and may have less or slower success than others might. At our best moments we hope people will have patience with us and give us a chance. But we don't expect them to simply excuse us or allow us to excuse ourselves from finding an approach to learning that can work for us.

Those with wiring that presents difficulties may need to do more self-discipline repetitions to gain some strength. But, no matter your biology or previous habit patterns, increasing your capacity for self-discipline will make changing more manageable. This is probable, whether you try to quit a bad or ineffective habit or want to incorporate a new way of doing something.

Don't Try to Do Too Much, But Do Enough

So, if it takes self-discipline to develop more self-discipline, you need to start small, tackle something that requires only a tad more discipline than you currently have and incrementally increase the challenges. Only after you've built your capacity to manage small daily temptations and impulses will you be ready to tackle more significant changes in your life—try waiting fifteen minutes before giving in to your craving for a snack; get dressed for the gym despite the inertia that feels like it's dragging you to a stop.

This doesn't mean you shouldn't take on a long-standing, irksome habit. You may already have the discipline capacity to implement a change, just don't set yourself up to inevitably fail again. Continually failing is a surefire way to kick the energy out of the motivation you need to manage change across the spectrum of your life responsibilities and down the long road of your lifespan.

Develop your self-discipline muscle slowly. Do lots of repetitions until you've built strength and then, if you are so inclined, you may go for a personal-best record on the discipline press. If you strain something while you're exercising your strength, you may be reluctant to continue the repetitions necessary to maintain your discipline fitness.

You need to have the patience to increase your challenge slowly. Increased capacity comes from challenges that create successes eighty percent of the time—the few failures show you're stretching your abilities, which causes growth. You must also plan to take time to recover—rest. It is during recovery time that the actual increase in capacity occurs. Self-discipline uses up brain energy, so eating and sleeping correctly also seem to help replenish your ability to keep at the process—very similar to physical workouts.

Exercising your self-discipline is pretty straightforward. First think about the challenges you already schedule in your day. You wouldn't do a hard gym workout the same day you have eighteen holes of golf booked with the club pro. Save most of the discipline energy you have for meeting your current challenges. Postpone larger challenges until you're rested, fed and have a moderate week ahead. For instance, you may decide to start a significant change in your diet when you have a week off.

There are benefits to including a few small practice times on most days. Maintaining a pattern of specific times for practice means the pattern will become a habit and that takes less energy than the effort to remember and initiate a workout .

Here are some good ways to begin to increase the strength and endurance of your self-control.

Make a Little Change

Push back against a small habit.

Forcing your brain to wake up and pay attention instead of letting it go on automatic takes self-discipline. Try enough repetitions of a new pattern and you'll be on the verge of establishing a new habit. Imagine the delight of having to choose a new habit to work on because the old one doesn't challenge you enough to increase self-discipline.

Some possibilities of small changes that can make your brain wake up:
- Spend five minutes thinking about tomorrow's projects.
- Resist checking emails or texts for a couple of minutes when you'd normally check them.
- Stall for five minutes when you want a snack, coffee, cigarette or a digital game.
- Park slightly farther away from your destination rather than closer.
- Take a different route to work.
- Stop swearing for a day.
- Brush your teeth with your opposite hand.
- Turn off the radio, music and videos and allow your world to be quiet for a few minutes while exercising, driving or walking.

There are thousands of other possibilities. Try ideas that feel interesting or valuable. Just keep them small and very doable. The idea is to practice light repetitions that require increased focus. Don't strain yourself.

Start a Very Simple New Activity

A lot of the benefit will come from remembering and doing a habit when you aren't used to it and then following through with repetitions. Try one or two you think would be useful.

- Get to work five minutes early.
- Look at your next day's calendar the night before.
- Always carry a notepad to list tasks you need to do—carry the pad; using it is optional.
- Read part of a professional journal article every workday.
- Get in bed fifteen minutes early.
- Floss one more day per week than you normally do.
- Brush your teeth for two minutes every night, or if you don't normally brush some nights, then brush for a minimum of thirty seconds every night.
- Walk to the far end of the block and back.
- Stretch for thirty seconds.
- Balance on each foot for fifteen seconds—can cause a dramatic increase in balance and decrease trips and falls.
- Get out of bed on weekdays without hitting the Snooze button.

Make the new activity very small, short and easy. If you haven't been doing it at all, start with as little as once or twice a day. As your success rate climbs above eighty percent, increase the challenge ten percent.

Don't Lose Track of Your Breathing

Keeping your attention on something as simple as breathing in and out encourages you to resist distractions. Resisting anything builds discipline. Each time your attention drifts to what has happened during your day or what's going to happen later on, refocus on your breathing. You're exercising your self-control. When noises or thoughts of emails seduce your attention away from awareness of your breath flowing in or out, just smile at yourself and return to noticing your breathing.

At the beginning, keep at it for thirty seconds. It's hard and what some people call your "monkey mind" will jump all over the place. Again, your capacity for discipline is strengthened by the effort more than the exact outcome. Put in the effort again and again—try it every two hours on the hour for thirty seconds—and you're gaining self-control. This is beyond any success you have with your breathing. Just remembering or responding to a reminder to do your breathing exercise will add to your willpower capacity.

Physical Activity Is Worth Bonus Points

Physical activity offers benefits to your brain. Exercise bathes your brain in growth chemicals, making change easier. This is especially true for remembering new information and creating new habits.

In addition, brain-growth chemicals seem to help stabilize mood and decrease impulsivity. A quieter brain, which is ready to change and remember, is the brain you want when you're trying to establish a new habit.

If you do one or some of the ideas below on a regular basis, they're worth bonus points.

- Do any physical activity for twenty minutes at least once a week—walk, climb stairs, bike, run, swim, resistance train, split wood, dance, yoga. Add days or time only when you've got a solid pattern established.
- Walk, run or wheel your chair at a pace that makes you aware that you're breathing a bit harder than usual, but where you can still talk or sing easily.
- Do arm curls with your grocery bags as you walk to your car.
- Hold on to a chair and do a few squats.
- Stand up from a chair with leg power alone.
- Walk around the room while you talk on the phone.

- Climb stairs instead of taking elevators or escalators.
- Walk or bike to the store or park as far away from your destination as time allows.
- Take items to the basement, attic, or garage one at a time instead of in one large load—what's known in our family as "gratuitous calorie burn".

By slowly increasing your bouts of self-discipline and upping the intensity and/or length of time, you'll build capacity for easier change. Changing will further increase your ability to change. You'll find yourself riding a positive spiral of change, ready to adapt to more of the opportunities you come across.

In his book *Elevate: An Essential Guide to Life,* Joseph Deitch, the founder and chairman of Commonwealth Financial Network, shares that after hundreds of times successfully remembering to appreciate, he began to forget. He credits those hundreds of previous appreciations with his ability to quickly resume an attitude of "thankfulness instead of dread and disdain." And Deitch tells his readers "to my astonishment and delight, my appreciation list started to include various annoyances and disturbances." He saw each problem, each irritant as an opportunity to look deeper, to find a solution, to examine what he could change about the situation or himself.

When you're comfortable changing, you'll be more effective convincing your employees and partners to try new ideas. Now there's another bonus plan.

Section 5: **Ways to Make Change Easier**

The habit you want to change is like a channel cut by a river. When you act without thinking, the channel will reliably keep you on the pre-worn course you established through numerous repetitions. Each recurrence deepens the route and assures that you'll have a predictable experience without investing any conscious effort—efficient, but not always in your best long-term interest.

In your brain, repetitions increase the insulation around neurons, stabilizing them and making them more resilient. Because of this, although the "dig a channel" metaphor is a great visual, maybe it should be changed to a metaphor that envisions a larger pipe with thicker walls.

If you're irritable, the odds are you don't remember the first time someone backed off in the face of your attitude and let you have your way. Now your irritability is an automatic pattern you unconsciously use to get your way. I suspect I've got a pretty well insulated pipe on this one. I've been working for years at alternative repetitions and I'm a lot less irritable than I was. Yet it still sneaks up on me when I'm surprised.

The first few times you gave subordinates tasks and then immediately explained explicitly how to do them, you were starting to build a habit for yourself and them. Now you automatically offer them your solution—like a crutch—even though you would prefer people learn to think for themselves.

 To reroute a habit, dig a new channel or enlarge a pipe takes conscious effort. Here are a few ways to minimize that effort and assure you're not wasting your time.

Repeat, Repeat and Repeat Again

The first rule of developing a new habit is to repeat, repeat, repeat and then repeat again and again. Repetitions strengthen the synaptic connections—dig the channel, build thicker walls on the pipe.

We have a major predisposition to save brain energy. Deliberately repeating an unfamiliar activity, in order to build a new behavior, takes brain energy. If you're trying to build a new habit, distraction, boredom or some other more pressing issues are likely to intervene and disrupt you long before the pattern is established. So stay vigilant.

Whatever you repeat often enough will become a permanent habit. Practice only creates the habit you want, if you practice each action or habit in the correct way enough times. If the repetitions are casually nestled into your established everyday routines, it's almost impossible to practice the new behavior flawlessly. Your habits have a cue that starts them—your coffee is brewing—and an unconscious action that automatically follows—you reach for the cereal box and pour cereal in the bowl.

If you're attempting to control some aspect of your habit like the amount of cereal you eat, you might decide to measure out one level cup each time, so you don't misjudge and pour too much. Unless you're paying particular attention, the old routine is likely to take over—reach for the box, open it, pour until the bowl looks full. The decision to measure will fall by the wayside, unless you're fully awake and paying close attention.

You've always bet more than you feel you should on March Madness basketball games. The office pool opens and you join in. In the excitement of the moment you do what you've always done—make a substantial bet on your choices. You'll need to pay close attention to climb out of the betting ditch before you join the pool.

A sports metaphor captures the process—learn the fundamentals, you want them to be second nature during the game. Or a musical one—practice scales until your fingers and ears can finally afford to focus exclusively on the emotion of the music. Or cooking—follow recipes until you are so familiar with the effects of ingredients and proportions that you can begin to improvise from scratch.

High-quality repetitions

The steps of a new habit need to be practiced in non-pressured situations where you have time to stop and repeat until the action is perfect and the flow is automatic. Ideally you'll make time to practice redoing small missteps until they're near perfect, before you try to deal with any variations.

- Script and practice giving an evaluation to a frustrating employee before you call them in.
- Find specific language to describe a positive trait of a team member before you try to toss an acknowledgement off the top of your head.

Set aside time

In order to build up the quantity of repetitions needed to develop your new habit, you'll need to set aside time to practice. Without time devoted specifically to deliberate practice, you're likely to simply drop one or two tries into your day at moments when you don't have the time to slowly do them right.

Those tries will most likely result in some successes and some failures. The failures will be repetitions of the wrong kind and will tend to reinforce the old, automatic habit you're trying to change. The chances of quickly building toward eventual success will diminish.

Have I mentioned repeating?

To succeed you need to repeat, repeat, repeat and then repeat again and again. If you have an important reason to learn a new habit—one that feels important to you—it will help motivate you to repeat that action in order to learn it correctly.

Past Experience Can Give You Motivation

I couldn't properly tack my sailboats in the most effective way, called a "roll tack," until I sat in my boat while it was attached to a dock and worked out where my hands needed to go—and repeated the move three or four dozen times. Then I cast off, sailed out on the lake and tried it. For the first time my hands just did what they needed to do. It felt like magic.

When I feel low-energy about learning something, I recall the great feeling that came directly out of the practice repetitions and I know what I need to do.

Another example:

I wanted to stop praising good work and instead acknowledge team members' growth as a step toward helping them internalize a sense of autonomy and become more self-directed—some call this "process praise."

I sat alone in my office and thought of any praise I'd recently given. Then I thought about what I wished I'd said and repeated it to myself a number of times. I amended numerous bits of praise, phrase by phrase.

Later that day I threw out a bit of acknowledgement to a team member, which nailed what I'd been practicing. It was great motivation to keep repeating the tutorial sessions with myself—repeating amended feedback until it was truly useable at appropriate moments.

Some quick examples:

- *That worked well* instead of *Good work*
- *Your approach is different than I've see anyone else try* instead of *You're really creative*
- *I noticed you were on time this morning* instead of *Nice work getting here on time*

Philosophy or a Saying Can Remind and Motivate

When I need to rein in my urge to move on to something more complex or to quiet my discouragement at how long something is taking to learn, I often repeat to myself, *Slow, deliberate practice will allow you to learn it the fastest*. This simple, clear statement captures my experience and understanding. It encourages me to slow down.

I try to be my own best coach and find the words that will motivate me to stick at whatever I'm trying to do. Here's one of my go-to motivational reminders.

> *Don't think, just get started. How good do you want to be?*

Whatever your passion—sports, business, music, dance, relationships—consider researching what the best coaches and teachers in your field say. Look for bits of wisdom about practice, repetition or basics.

One of basketball's most successful coaches, John Wooden, is known for how hard he worked to create carefully designed, perfect practices. One could learn a lot from exploring his philosophy. Check out any of the books he authored or coauthored in his lifetime.

Positive self-talk leads you forward. Negative talk focuses you back. Keep it upbeat.

Slow Down

If you're trying to repeat a successful action enough times to enshrine it as a new habit, you might casually rip through hundreds of repetitions of mixed quality. But the number of correct tries might be minimal and might well be overwhelmed by the number of incorrect attempts. A few dozen successes mixed in with dozens of partial failures or not-quite-right attempts will not create change like a few dozen repetitions done just right.

To do things correctly you need to slow down and pay attention to small details. You need to both slow down the actions and slow down your overall time schedule.

You know you're at about the right speed when you have perfect success over eighty percent of the time and you have plenty of time to slow down and try again. Too ambitious a schedule to implement a new habit will cause stress, and that distraction will almost assuredly impede your practice.

> Imagine you've decided to change the way you assign tasks. You want to encourage your employees to ask questions and think for themselves rather than simply giving them all the information you can imagine they might need. The next time you handoff a task, you ask, "What else do you want to know?" They say, "All set!" But that doesn't end up being true.

> You sit quietly and think of a few specific questions that might have opened up the conversation more and encouraged the team member to think the task through. You try a few out loud and modify them a bit so that the questions will come out naturally and easily even if you're rushed.

> The next time you give a task you say, "I'm sure there are questions. What do we need to talk about?" And if they say, "All

set?" You might ask, "Where are the risk points?" Your approach didn't quite get you what you wanted, but you are beginning to slow things down and closing in on an effective approach. Taking time upfront may save you time and energy later.

To practice how to delegate tasks effectively, you need to think about questions that will lead toward outcomes you want. Now practice saying them out loud until you have them at your fingertips when you need them. Slow down. Take time to plan. Slow will save you time.

One way to slow things down is to take smaller steps.

> Your meetings wander and end up taking more time than you think they should. Part of the problem is you have a vague agenda, but mostly you feel it's hard to interrupt discussions that tend to get pretty far off the main point.
>
> To tighten up your meetings and keep them on task you decide to start off with a clear statement about sticking to the agenda and ending on time. For the next couple of meetings you make the statement but things still end up going astray. You realize that you need to make a stronger statement, one that encourages the rest of the participants to help reach your outcomes.
>
> You craft an opening: "We're all busy and don't need to waste our valuable time listening to each department hash out its piece of a project. When I feel that we're in danger of getting off track, I'm going to restate the question we need to address as a group. If there are specific questions that may need an additional meeting, we'll note them and move on."

As you start the next meeting, you reach for the right words and stumble a bit. It doesn't sound clear or authoritative even to your ear. You crafted an opening, but you didn't practice it enough. Running through it a few times felt like practice, but you needed to slow down and memorize certain phrases—particularly the opening: "We are all busy." Using both "busy" and "valuable time" repeats the central point and means more people are likely to remember it.

The next time, you memorize three key phrases you want to use during your opening, and you're clearer. You also feel more comfortable and are able to interrupt more quickly.

This scripting and memorizing may feel stilted, but it has immense value when you have a repeating pattern that you don't seem able to change by mere awareness. The professional speakers you enjoy are actually giving carefully scripted talks. Comedians check out their laugh lines and tweak their words again and again to achieve those quick, spontaneous moments that surprise and feel so naturally funny to us.

Having a clear reason to change, then slowing down and repeating creates faster learning and superior results.

Be Clear About What You Want to Accomplish

Change is a project in and of itself and you need a clear goal or outcome to efficiently move a project toward success. Success is defined by the outcome you have. For many of my clients, it's fun to wander through a garden of possibilities, to see if an idea will appear or take shape. In that case think of the outcome as trying to find new ideas.

Sometimes, when you ask yourself what outcome you want, the answer will be too simple. What outcome were you looking for as you worked on the opening statement for the meeting? *I wanted a clear sentence.* While that's true, the more important question is to figure out why you want a clear sentence? *So everyone is clear about what we're trying to do.*

Drilling down to the most important outcome is often getting to the most long-range goal—you want the meeting to be more productive, to waste less time, to encourage more forward motion on team projects.

Knowing what you want both focuses and motivates. The focus means less wasted energy and the motivation can lead to a willingness to invest more of your time in quality practice repetitions.

We tend to move toward what we are looking at. Having a clear outcome in mind will constantly nudge you toward the path that leads to that goal. The more important and meaningful the goal the more likely you or your team are to invest additional energy in the project. So having a notable, clear goal weights the balance toward success.

As you get started, ask yourself what you want to have accomplished when you're done. This bigger or overall accomplishment is more powerful than a smaller goal like, to practice or take the next step in your change project.

The outcome of your practice ahead of the meeting is to make the meetings more productive in less time. Some of the specific actions you'll need to take or practice are—script some phrases that explain clearly what you're going to do, practice the phrases multiple times out loud, practice the phrases in the context of complete thoughts.

One of my clients was good at encouraging her team members, but fell into inadvertently harsh slams when correcting them. She was clear, her goal for the team was for them to learn effective sales strategies, in addition she wanted strong professional relationships with them. She practiced avoiding impulsive critiques that distracted people from her messages of strategic quality. In just one week she went from: "That's stupid! You can do better." to "When you're talking with a customer, be sure to begin your conversation with something important to them."

It can be straightforward to figure out the action or question you want to practice, but it's often more important that first you're perfectly clear what outcome you're trying to accomplish.

Imagine the Details and Your Actions Will Follow

What you plan and practice in your head has a greater chance of occurring in real time when you need it. This isn't the wishful thinking of some far out psychic charlatan. Research shows that visual and mental practice helps athletes, presenters, managers and others improve the way they think and feel.

It works because thinking builds brain pathways the same way doing does. When we think, the brain areas that control muscles—including your speech—create micro twitches. These twitches are small versions of the larger contractions and twitches that generate actions.

Carefully plan and practice your thinking. It will build your capacity to more easily generate new thoughts in the middle of an interaction, do a new activity more smoothly and even feel differently than you would normally feel in a particular situation.

Try these activities to help integrate change into your life:

- Before a presentation or difficult conversation briefly outline key phrases that communicate your important points. Now sit back and imagine the situation in detail and repeat the phrases you've created. You're more likely to end the interaction having said what you wanted.
- If you decide to start checking your task-list or calendar more often, picture the circumstances where you'll do that. Try to picture details of time, place and method.
- If you have a hard time remembering names of people you meet, picture meeting someone and using their name at least three times. *Hello, I'm Bob… Good to meet you Jane. So, Jane, how can I be of help? It was good to meet you Jane.* By picturing the interaction and practicing the ways you'll repeat a name, you're much more likely to do exactly that the next time you meet someone new.
- If you're trying to change a physical activity—e.g., grab your cell phone when you leave the office—create a new routine and practice it in your head. Picture the small details of getting ready to leave and insert the new activity in the place you want it. Your muscles are more likely to reach for the phone and your brain is more likely to whisper in your ear, *Don't forget your phone.*
- You can also use this technique to improve your athletic, musical or keyboard skills.

Practice is key to change. You can practice in your head or in the physical world. The practice you do in your head can get you up to speed without alerting others that you're practicing. Try it.

Don't Redecide

It's very difficult to contain impulsive tendencies when we're buffeted by short-term conflicting emotions and temptations.

A clear, definite choice made with care and then remade when you're tired, hungry, feeling sexual or irritated is a setup for failure. This re-choice is highly likely to be a short-term, impulsive reaction rather than based on careful consideration of your long-term best interests.

In answer to your sleepy-self asking whether you need to get up right now or can snooze for 15 more minutes, the only answer you should give is a continually repeated reminder that, *I already decided this is the time to get up, so get up!*

If you see chocolate and think, *I can have one piece.* Start repeating, *I decided to not have any sweets until after dinner, so move on!*

It's important to refute the feeling that there's an opportunity to redecide. The repetition of the thought *I've already decided!* helps to block insubordinate thoughts, images and feeling that are encouraging you to think there's an opportunity to redecide.

The process needs to be very deliberate.

- Make a clear, unequivocal decision.

- Think through the likely re-decision points—e.g., the alarm goes off, the chocolate calls.
- Decide what you're going to say to block the false notion that it's okay to redecide, and practice it—*Just keep moving! Is what I use.*
- When you falter, start repeating the phrase in your head to block tempting thoughts.
- Act on your decision before the pressure to redecide has a chance to take hold.
- Celebrate your willpower!
- Rededicate yourself to not redeciding the next time.

Redeciding is a major factor in failure to stick to new behaviors. Any equivocations will sabotage your efforts. Be very clear and definite. Don't look back! Don't redecide!

Track Your Habits

Formally making a check mark on a chart—or some other clear indication that you have achieved a small success—can have a powerful effect on your future rate of success. Even tracking your rate of "failure" can help raise your awareness. This may be one of the simplest ways to nudge yourself toward change.

Make a simple chart with days of the week down the rows with successive weeks noted across the columns. Each time you remember to try a new action—floss your teeth—or repeat the old habit—have dessert—make a mark.

Formally noting an activity creates awareness. Awareness produces a slight hesitation in a habitual activity. A slight hesitation makes a small opening for you to institute an alternative activity. Awareness after an activity generates a moment where you can savor success. Savoring reinforces the new pattern.

The next encouragement may seem a bit silly but seems to help. Carefully choose the style of mark you want to make. Some people prefer a checkmark, others like small, filled-in circles or slash mark. Surprisingly, choosing a mark that gives you a small bit of satisfaction is motivating. The same thing is true for the style of chart—set it up so it gives your eye pleasure and you're a bit more likely to use it regularly.

It is also important to keep your chart simple and easy to both see and access. Keep the marker right next to it and keep the chart wherever you are most likely to perform the activity. For instance, keep something in your pocket if you're tracking cigarettes or food intake, but post it on the mirror if that's where you brush or floss. In your pocket will also be most helpful if you're trying to get on top of a habit that occurs at random places—i.e. ineffective attitude or style of interaction with team members.

If you use an app to capture your marks, use an easy to access one—a calendar or note that's one touch away is best. Complex systems look great but are often too many touches or swipes away to remain useful.

Savor Successes

As you try to institute any new habit you need to emphasize as many successes as possible because initially there may only be a few. Take time to savor that you remembered to try or that your effort went better than usual.

Savoring can be as simple and enjoyable as choosing a success you've had and spending some time enjoying the feeling of success. Remembering an event after it happens affects your brain similarly to having the actual experience. If nothing seems important enough to spend time reliving, you're probably being a bit hard on yourself. Try to focus on small improvements or on the fact you got in a few good repetitions.

If you feel you haven't had a success since you decided to begin changing, then think back to an earlier time when you came close to what you're striving for. It's fine to start wherever you find a positive experience.

To get the most out of savoring, you need to focus on vivid details and positive emotions you experienced. Remembering vivid physical, emotional and action details builds a realistic recreation of the original experience. Pay particular attention to smells as they're some of our most powerful doorways back to memories. Of course when your success happened in the hallway at the office there may not be many distinguishing smells so also look for visual or tactile details and sounds.

Emotions are another anchor to past experiences. It isn't necessary to just remember strong emotions. Smaller ones are more common and work quite well. It's an interesting phenomenon that pleasurable emotions often slide by us and we jump to a negative feeling. Positive emotions open us up to changes and are most important to reconnect with.

Positive emotions include simple pleasure like what you feel when you make a sale, treat a difficult condition, meet an old friend or solve a problem for a team member. Satisfaction is another quiet feeling that gets overlooked. Satisfaction is often described as a bit of warmth or pride. It is an important emotion to recognize when you want to recall successes.

Our cultural definition of emotions has put a premium on large powerful emotions and those that surface most often in relationships. This lexicon often ends up ignoring or devaluing some of the emotions that many people feel. There isn't a sports fan around that doesn't go through a string of emotions nearly every game. Every business person feels subtle or serious anxiety on a regular basis. Stress is an indication of emotion. Any of these emotions can help anchor you to a past situation where you were successful.

A word of caution is in order. Just as savoring is a powerful way to increase the ratio of positive experiences, if you spend too much time thinking about past negative experiences you underline and boost old patterns, unwanted activities and stressful emotions— none of which helps you change.

If you catch yourself replaying a failure or slip back to an old habit or other negative experience, use that as a cue to dig up a positive success to savor. Co-opt the negative to work for you to build the new habit.

Hesitate to Share Your Goals

To get tasks accomplished, it's common to try to find ways to force ourselves into being accountable to others. Research suggests that this approach may be less helpful when striving for larger goals. Many individuals make more progress when they hold their aspirations close and don't share.

My experience is that quietly working toward a goal may help keep resistance lower. When we share what we're trying to do, our failures are more public and our discouragement or embarrassment may be higher. Instead of motivating it becomes discouraging. It's hard for us to appreciate that failures are an important aspect of success.

There's nothing wrong with sharing with a coach or a friend who is passionately non-judgmental, who historically celebrates small successes and who will never disrespect your efforts whether they lead to success or setback.

But if you're looking for easy ways to tilt the chances of success in your favor, start your change process quietly and only share with one or two neutral people. Or share the factual step you're taking not the dream you're trying to realize, *I'm trying to write every day.* Rather than, *I'm writing a book.*

Show what you're doing instead of telling what you want to do. We all respect what we see more than we respect what people tell us they dream about doing.

If you have solidified changes that you feel aren't being recognized, it's essential that you draw your supervisor's attention to your change. When you feel sure that you are able to maintain the change, ask in a curious tone "I've been trying to send much more succinct emails. I feel I've had some success. Is that your impression?" "I've been focusing on trying to come up with my own solution before I just ask how to do things. Would you keep an eye on that and give me your feedback in a week or so?"

A cautionary note: Manage your image. Control your reputation. Don't set yourself up by promising until you are truly ready to deliver.

Outside coaches can be particularly helpful in supporting changes in team members. A coach can help the employee, or you, design an approach to change that utilizes strengths and personalizes goals so they offer private satisfaction and aren't just half-hearted responses to the demands of the work environment.

A coach might help articulate a goal that is private but that also leads to meeting a supervisor's concerns. Try keeping the private goal in yourself until and unless you feel it has an appropriate place in the work conversation.

Practice and Repeat

Just thought I'd mention these again as they're hugely important to your success. Practice! Repeat!

Section 6: **Change with Almost No Effort**

Self-discipline is an important component of change, but in certain circumstances you can alter your behavior without using much precious discipline-energy.

If you adjust the way you arrange your organization systems, office or car, you might be able to institute changes with very little effort or awareness.

Change Your Physical Environment

Try to physically place things so that the habit you're trying to develop has no roadblocks. When you feel an urge, you want to be able to act with next to no effort, no thought, no decisions and very little chance you'll get detoured.

- **Goal**: Keep a to-do list
  Physical Change: Keep your to-do list within the easy-reach zone on top of your desk, in your pocket or on your phone. Have the most current items visible so you don't have pages to turn or screens to click through. If you plan to use paper, always keep a pen where you can easily reach it. If your list is electronic, keep it open and waiting, certainly no more than one click away.

- **Goal**: Exercise regularly
  Physical Change: Keep your workout clothes out and visible, your socks with your shoes, shirt with your shorts or pants. If the weather is getting cool, keep your shell with the rest of your clothes. My wife gets to the gym more often because she keeps an extra set of workout clothes, sneakers and a yoga mat in her car.

- **Goal**: Pay bills on time
  Physical Change: Put bills to be paid in a prominent place with a large label where they'll be visible from a regular route you use in your office or home. The best place is often right next to the place you're going to pay them.

- **Goal**: Start online work you've resisted doing
  Physical Change: Put a prominent link on your computer or smartphone for any online task you might resist doing.

Use the opposite approach when you're trying to break a current habit.

- **Goal**: Eat fewer unhealthy snacks
  Physical Change: Place snack items where they're not easily visible or reachable—think not obvious, not handy, inconvenient. You're more likely to eat less if you have to dig for them. Place them at the back of the office fridge, in a closed cabinet or drawer out of reach from your desk.

- **Goal**: Ignore email when concentrating
  Physical Change: Turn off email, text and social media alerts during intensive work spurts. This is equivalent to making them less visible.

- **Goal**: Don't get caught by the Internet
  Physical Change: Delete any "favorites," desktop links or other saved links that lead to entertaining or distracting web addresses. The little extra effort of having to type the address will slow down your impulse to visit the site.

Make Choosing Easy

If a certain decision is optimal, make that choice the easiest one to make.

- **Goal**: Help employees save more
  Change: Change benefit questionnaires to increase compliance. Most U.S. employees are not that good at saving through their 401(k) plans. Yet some companies are able to dramatically increase the number who voluntarily save a portion of their paycheck by simply requiring them to opt out of the company saving plan if they wish, instead of asking them to choose to sign up—opt in. Do nothing and they automatically save.

- **Goal**: Reduce sick days
  Change: Make the procedure for calling in sick just a bit more involved. Require a personal phone call instead of an email or text. It's more challenging and brings up a tad more inhibition when employees aren't truly ill.

- **Goal**: Waste less time
  Change: Set up your computer's default settings to lead you to your task list or calendar, not your email or browser. Keep a clock in full view while you work. Track your hours each day or each project.

- **Goal**: Have more focused meetings
  Change: Shorten meeting times by default. Things that are better managed through email or within a specific department will tend to migrate off the agenda. If the default is short, it becomes slightly more difficult to schedule longer meetings.

- **Goal**: Stop micromanaging
  Change: Set a clear check-in date or time—even daily—at the start of the project, then put materials about the project out of sight and ask not to be cc'd on routine communications.

Make Your Organizing Tools Easy to Use

Locate the tools you use to organize yourself so that they're waiting for you, calling out to you, nudging you as you walk by.

- **Goal**: Deal with in-box items
  Change: Place the tray or box you use to capture incoming paper notes or mail in a location that you pass as you enter your office.

- **Goal**: Be on time
  Change: Place a clock or timer in your direct line of sight. Don't force yourself to look right or left. A phone in your pocket on in resting mode with a blank screen creates a small obstacle to noticing the time and is less likely to grab your awareness.

- **Goal**: Don't forget your phone, keys
  Change: Place a dish to hold your phone and keys right in the path you use to walk out of the office or house—on a table, counter or even the floor.

- **Goal**: Put every responsibility you have on your task list
  Change: By default keep your task list open—one click or one touch away.

Your goal is to conserve as much of your self-discipline energy as possible. Remembering takes energy, deciding takes energy, resisting takes energy. When you're trying to initiate a new habit or procedure, always ask, *How can I make this automatic, so easy I'll tend to just do it?*

Section 7: **Keep Your Resistance in Check**

Change and resistance often go hand in hand. You may completely ignore or halfheartedly attempt to follow other peoples' advice. But you may also not be good about doing many of those things you decide are important to you.

Your Resistance May be Protecting You

The very habits we want to change are often protecting important objectives, which we are may be unaware we even have.

I want to learn to speak up, but I want people to like me. It doesn't make sense to speak up if it might upset someone. Speaking up might threaten my comfort and potentially threaten an important tenet of my approach to life—people should try to get along and not create discomfort for others.

I want to get projects done on time. But taking the time to 'organize' my projects and tasks is a waste of time because I could be doing something 'productive.'

I want to give my employees more autonomy, but it's important that people know I can do everything.

I want to increase company assets to provide additional stability, but I see myself as a bold instigator of new projects.

I want to stop smoking, but smoking helps me relax and not be so tense around other people.

I want to stop drinking too much, but alcohol helps me fit in and build relationships that I crave.

> *I want to stop blowing up, but blowing up helps me get people's attention when they're doing stupid things.*
>
> *I want to be more open to new ideas from other people, but I don't want to appear as if I don't know things.*

The protective aspect of your resistance to change may shield you from the discomfort of doing something unfamiliar or from investing additional energy and attention to do something new. It may also assure you'll continue doing what feels important.

- If you believe that creativity and spontaneity are linked, you may resist trying to deliberately structure and use your task list. Structuring your tasks may unconsciously feel like you are abandoning your creativity. Similarly, writing things down may feel like an admission that your memory isn't good.
- If being out of shape prevents you from competing in your sport of choice, and you think losing at a competition says something bigger about your overall capabilities, you might find yourself resisting workouts and therefore avoiding the perils of competition.
- If the people you work with are blunt, pushy, passionate or express negative emotions strongly, you may not control your irritation. You don't want to appear like a wimp.

Identify resistive tendencies that may be working at cross-purposes to your stated goals. Change may not occur just because you realize there are unseen benefits to your "bad" habit, but recognizing those tendencies will certainly make it easier to construct a strategy to create a new habit. You increase the odds that you'll also be more motivated and persistent about trying despite setbacks.

Most unconscious purposes aren't that hard to discover. A few well-placed questions from someone experienced in the complexity of human motivations and ideas can help increase your awareness. And it's possible that you already have a hint about what's going on. When your motivations are named, you are likely to nod or chuckle at how obvious they are.

> A client of mine, the owner of a small manufacturing plant, couldn't get himself to stay away on weekends, and he never took vacations. He said to me, "I know I should get away but I just feel pulled to check in at the plant." I asked if his managers were capable of running it without him and he said they were.
>
> "I try to stay away. I just have to check in," he repeated.
>
> It took a number of sessions and lots of questions that attempted to dig down below his level of self-observation before he and I got at the root of his resistance. He needed to feel necessary. His whole value as an owner was based on his ability to fix anything, answer any questions and still be seen as one of the guys. If he wasn't there, his value might slip. He was there to keep an eye on his image and hold his place in the flow of work.

If you want to take a crack at finding the missing piece of your resistance puzzle, try asking yourself, *What advantage might there possibly be to doing things this way?* Or, *If I started doing things differently, what would people think?*

Knowing your hidden beliefs may not eliminate your resistance, but it may weaken it significantly and give you a target to focus your best thinking on. You might realize that, *At some point it may have been important that I not ask questions because it made me feel like people would think I didn't know things I should know. But now it's important that I model for my people how to ask themselves and others important questions.*

Welcome Discomfort

Resistance can also protect you from the uncertainties and discomfort of transitioning from what you know to what you don't know. Transitions take us through a series of steps or states of mind. We move from comfort and knowing through a period of discomfort and not knowing, and then back again to a new knowing and the comfort that comes with it.

It is tough to decide to step voluntarily into the chaotic, unpredictable feelings that can occur during a transition from an old to a new habit. Even the potential discomfort that may be coming can easily kick your protective resistance into action.

A transition can be sped up by deliberately practicing the new habit. Knowing that the time of discomfort between the ease of an old habit and the ease of a new habit is limited, can give you more confidence to step into the unknown. Information and courage are two antidotes to resistance.

Most of us invest a lot of effort avoiding uncomfortable feelings, physical stress, confusion, etc. Change requires discomfort. A nice example of this phenomenon is exercising to build additional physical strength or endurance. To gain capacity you have to literally create small tears in your muscles. The muscles then "super compensate" to prepare you for the next physical challenge. Of course you have to avoid larger injuries. Gaining the experience to know the difference is a key skill.

Similarly, pushing yourself to do things that feel emotionally or intellectually uncomfortable can help you be better prepared for the next uncomfortable challenge. Push yourself to change a small habit and you're a bit more equipped for whatever you need to change next. Tolerate a dose of discomfort and you'll judge the next dose as a bit less uncomfortable.

Welcome discomfort as a harbinger of change—physical, emotional and intellectual change. Discomfort may also accompany changes in your business—new personnel, new processes, new services, new products, new thinking in your field, etc.

If you're resistant to feeling uncomfortable, you'll likely stay stuck in your old habits. Resistance to experiencing discomfort is a major reason people don't pursue changes. If you claim you're bored, I'd say that's an uncomfortable feeling you need be willing to push into. Feel distracted? Chances are you're avoiding some feeling the project you're distracted from brings up. Feeling lazy? Entertainment or zoning is less likely to demand discipline.

Other Things You Can Try
When You've Set Goals and Haven't Followed Through

- The advice in section 5 on not redeciding is helpful when you feel resistance to following through on a commitment you've made. Decide what your next step is during a non-emotional, non-tired, non-distracted time and then don't redecide. Just do it!
- Implement a change or new habit in even smaller steps than you've tried before. Try to stir up as little stress as possible. Before you start trying to keep a detailed task list, try updating your project list once a week. Open and roughly title a new document as a first step into that report you've been resisting. Start eating a few more vegetables before you try cutting back on sweets.
- Build up your willpower with small challenges before you try a particularly onerous change.
- Find and use an appealing reward when you take a crack at a tough change and get some results.

Many people who I work with feel stuck and unable to change. Most often they talk about resisting their own attempts to change. Resistance is frustrating, but it isn't insurmountable. Like most aspects of change, resistance can be thought through, strategized against and effective approaches to fight it can practiced. But you're most likely to succeed if your reasons for trying to change are internally important to you, not simply a response to external demands to change—someone else or circumstances insisting you do it.

Do It for Yourself

When we understand at an emotional and cognitive level why we're working at a specific change, we carry extra motivating force into the game. Doing it for others, if they're truly important to us, may be enough, but be certain that your relationship with them is essential to your goals in life.

Think through your motivation very carefully. What's in it for you?

> *I'll feel better.*

> *It's something I think is important.*

> *I want them to like me—owe me, hire me, work for me, etc.*

> *I've dreamed of doing it for a long time.*

Any of these might be important, but so might changing for a more practical goal.

> A salesman client of mine reported that he wanted to make more money. But each time he got close to meeting a sales level that would have given him a bonus he "got tired and lost my drive." I asked him why he wanted money.

> He answered quickly, "To provide more things for my family."

> "Do they need anything in particular?" I asked.

> "Not really, but my wife would like us to save more."

"Do you want to save?"

"I don't really care, but I want to do it for her."

"What would *you* like?"

"What do you mean?" He seemed genuinely puzzled.

"Is there something you would find really interesting or fun that would take more money? It could be a thing or an activity or vacation."

"Sure, I'd like a new car. I spend all day in my car, and it would be fun to have a better one with a good sound system and a hands-free phone connection."

"Would that be worth pushing to break through to the next sales level, to earn a bonus so you could get a car?"

When we talked more about a car and resolving the issues he would need to clarify with his wife, he became progressively more excited that he might be able to do it. His resistance had been tied to pleasing other people and having to ignore his own desires. Pleasing his wife wasn't crucial—she liked him already.

If you've had troubles all your life getting things done, being places on time, paying attention to details, forgetting things like your keys, cell phone or homework at crucial moments, then you likely have also spent your life hearing criticism from other people.

It's essential for all of us to find a reason to change that's important to us personally, but it's particularly important for those carrying lots of memories of past criticism.

Persistence is Resistance's Conqueror

You might attempt to reframe resistance as proof of persistence. Resistance can be thought of as persistently continuing an old approach or a behavior. Your ongoing resistance is a reflection that you're also persistent about pushing into a change—if you didn't persist there would be no reason to resist.

Thinking of yourself as persistent may well be more encouraging than labeling yourself as resistant. Resistant may feel like not changing where persistent may feel like not quitting.

You have persistence—use it to focus positively on implementing a new habit or system.

Call It Names

One way to work your way around resistance is to mock it as a lightweight, or deride what your resistance says to you as lies—it may be best to keep all this to yourself. Imagine trying to get your tired body out of bed to exercise and you feel yourself slipping into the grip of resistance. Try thinking/saying any of the following:

> *No chance this fly-weight, wimp resistance is going to keep me in bed. It's such a phony that all I have to do is get my feet on the floor and it's beaten. It thinks it's a tough guy when I'm flat on my back, but if I put on my exercise gear, it's no tougher than a piece of tissue paper.*

> *Sure, I rarely get started early on projects, but this voice that says I can't change is just smoke my resistance is blowing in my ear. All I have to do is open the documents and work for five minutes and I've proven this feeling is phony.*

Most of us have an internal voice that lies to us about something. People who are struggling with addiction often have a voice that encourages them to use or drink, and that voice lies about the consequences. Any strong feeling might create a voice in your head. Beware when you're tired, hungry, angry, in love or in any other high-intensity feeling state. Don't believe everything you hear!

Your amygdala is the center of your emotions, and it can be a great place to focus your derision. *Hey, Amygdala, quit lying to me!* Choose the approach that spikes your emotions enough to give you energy to resist. *You lying piece of crap!* is acceptable in your head, unless it spikes your adrenaline too much and you find it escaping from the confines of your head and into your external world where you need to be much more professional or parental. If anger spills into your professional or personal world, tone down your disdain. Confront your resistance a bit more gently, *You're lying to me again!*

Just Act

When you feel lethargy and inertia sapping your willpower, try just moving—get on your feet, push your wheelchair a few feet, pick up your gym bag, start typing on your report. Action fights passive resistance. Create momentum by just acting.

There's no need to know what you're going to do once you're moving. Just move! After that, if you're still stuck, you might try taking another step or a short walk. But even if you just act, you're more likely to eventually move in a productive direction than if you're not moving.

Hire a Professional Resistance Fighter

It's easy to blame yourself when you feel resistant, but blame usually isn't very effective at moving resistance aside. It's difficult to get moving toward your goal when you're feeling resistive. When you're stuck, a professional coach or a support group may be the answer.

Good, experienced coaches have stood toe-to-toe with resistance many times and backed it down. Think of it as a judo match in which resistance's energy is used to unbalance it. An expert will use your own resistance to motivate you to change. A little push in the right place and resistance often shows just how laughably weak it is.

An experienced coach can be a great cheerleader, corner person, and... well, coach.

Resistance Can be a Good Sign

You might also think about your resistance as a sign you're working on an area that is worthwhile. If you're trying to replace an unhelpful habit with a healthy one, the resistance is a sign of just how deeply embedded and important the habit is. Resistance means you're doing valuable work. Congratulations, you're not fooling around!

Now surprise your resistance by trying a different approach. Maybe start resisting all efforts to fall back into your old habit.

Section 8: **Temper Your Emotional Reactions**

You are who you are, right?

You really can't change your fundamental personality, right?

If you react without thinking, that's just the way you are, right?

The answers are, of course, "false" on all accounts. Even the most fundamental aspects of your reactions can be changed with a new frame of mind, specific goals, effective techniques and sufficient practice.

I recently read a piece of intriguing research. Our behavior and our environment can change certain aspects of our DNA. That certainly stands on its head the notion of not being able to change. I'll concede that you're likely to face a long, arduous task, if you start working on extensive, comprehensive, complex changes in your personality—this is what lifetimes are for. But specific, discrete, simple changes are absolutely doable in a moderate space of time. And a series of small, specific changes can add up pretty quickly to some fundamental changes.

Of all the things that people bemoan as too difficult to change, hot, negative emotional reactions to feelings of frustration, irritation or aggression lie near the top of the list. But these reactions are also changeable. And it's a good thing because they're extraordinarily unprofessional habits and many business owners and professional-practice leaders unconsciously dump them on employees.

> I once worked with the owner of a small trucking firm. He ran the business successfully, but his real joy was selling services, not managing drivers.
>
> He made his margins by hiring young drivers, but with their lower wages came demands for training and closer supervision. He wanted to be on the road bringing in new accounts, instead he

had to make calls to get hungover young men out of bed, worry that drivers couldn't follow directions to a new client—pre-GPS—and constantly answer customers' inquiries about delivery times.

When things went wrong he berated his drivers for not paying attention. Once he started in, he got loud quickly. Even clients commented on the yelling they heard in the background on phone calls.

He rebuffed my concerns that he sounded unprofessional with "They won't think unless I beat it into their heads." I asked if he really wanted to be yelling and he said, "No. But it just comes out. I can't control it when I'm frustrated."

I stood up, bent toward him and yelled, "Just quit it! You sound like a jerk!"

He stared at me, confused and shocked. I asked him if that would make him stop yelling. He broke into an ear to ear grin and quietly responded, "You know, it just might."

Next time I came in I asked if he had yelled during the week and he admitted he had. "But less than normal," he added.

"Would it help if I yelled again?"

"No. You just sound stupid. But what am I supposed to do when I'm frustrated?"

We developed a plan where he would call in his number-two person when something wasn't right and ask him to fix it. He also decided that it was more professional to walk away than to yell and to practice visualizing himself out on his boat on a hot summer day.

If you react toward your team or colleagues with anger, sarcasm or derision, you need to change that behavior—period! It's unprofessional, disrespectful, gets in the way of your team's learning and will convince the best people to find a better boss. Here's how you can use basic techniques to stop it.

Rehearse What You Want to Do and Be

Brains change throughout our lives. There is no reason to accept who you are at any given time as the final draft of your personality. Although most adults see themselves as unchangeable—except for minor decorative touches or inevitable decay—there are thousands of people over the age of eighty who are demonstrating what neuroscience is also proving, growing and changing are possible at any age.

A good first step to reframe the issue is to let go of "I can't change" and try "If I want to and I practice, I can begin to change."

There are many validated reports confirming that people can control their most fundamental bodily reactions. During no-anesthesia surgery people control their pain and bleeding. With practice, breathing and heart rate can be slowed to the point where, in some cases, people are mistaken for dead. The sensation of taste is also manageable. People can eat foul-tasting substances with delight. It's possible to learn to keep your body warm in freezing conditions. World-class athletes learn to regulate their anxiety, calm themselves down or psych themselves up depending on what will help them perform at their best.

Most of us haven't been introduced to these techniques that can moderate many of our physical and emotional reactions. These approaches aren't magic, they aren't spiritual and they aren't mystical. They're possible—and unlike some people's claim that they can levitate, they're reproducible in scientific experiments. You don't need to believe in them. You can try them and discover whether they work for you. What does this have to do with emotions?

It's very possible to learn to regulate your emotional reactions—to quiet anxiety, to soothe your own irritation, to respond with respect to those who haven't given you much. If personal or business productivity and effectiveness would be enhanced by an different emotional reaction than the one you automatically use, you can train yourself to use the better reaction.

The first step is to stop repeating questionable "facts"—many times the facts only feel true because you've heard and said them so often. Just because something is traditional—"You can't change who you fundamentally are"—doesn't make it true. Those who made up and passed along old sayings are no more likely to be wise or correct than you and I are, so don't take their sayings on faith—test them. Many common sense ideas are seductive because they allow us to get off the hook—"Old dogs can't learn new tricks. Who wouldn't want to believe that? It gives me permission to stop trying to improve.

Repeating cliché phrases or sayings actually gets in your way of thinking. Cults teach members "thought-stopping" techniques to keep them from listening to other points of view or thinking for themselves—if a notion that threatens the accepted way of thinking is introduced by someone, members are encouraged to chant, pray or repeat a mantra to stop themselves from thinking about the possibility of any way except the group's way.

So stop blocking the notion that you can change. Stop repeating sayings that inhibit your ability to feel hopeful about changing.

By the way, I was a leading dog trainer once upon a time. Old dogs can learn new tricks, if they've been kept in practice by learning new things throughout their lives. If they haven't practiced, they can still learn. It just takes a little more patience while they get back into practice.

In fact, old dogs often learn more easily than puppies who are distracted and don't have a base of information to relate new learning to. Repeat after me, "You *can* teach old dogs new tricks."

Take 100% Responsibility for Changing

If you hold someone else responsible for your emotional reactions, you're unlikely to change.

> During World War II, a Jewish prisoner in a Nazi concentration camp watched the reactions of all the prisoners to their horrendous mistreatment by guards. He saw two reactions. Some prisoners became so survival-oriented that they acted like little more than greedy dogs, and in the insanity the Nazis cultivated, who could blame them.
>
> But other prisoners refused to give up their humanity in the face of the hopeless abuses. They continued to respond with compassion and dignity both to each other and in some cases to the guards. These latter individuals had no physical control of their circumstances or lives, but understood that they still had the ability and responsibility to control their own reactions. After surviving the camps, the observer, Victor Frankel, became a renowned psychiatrist and proponent of taking responsibility for our emotional reactions.

If concentration-camp prisoners can find a way to take responsibility for the tiny aspect of their world that they have control over, we certainly can accept responsibility for our reactions to mild irritants.

It's easy to point the blame for irritation at the source of the immediate irritant. It's even somewhat reasonable to cast responsibility for our anger or upset at the person who is acting unreasonably. The problem is that this deflection of responsibility to others is not helpful or realistic.

They may be responsible for their actions, but not for our reactions to them. Our reactions are our responsibility.

When you get irritated at others, you may assume it's their fault for being so irresponsible or annoying. But consider how irritable you are to police officers or bosses who are also annoying? With those individuals and with investors, clients, your in-laws, etc., you probably are able to control your reactions. In fact, you can most likely make an extensive list of situations where you control your irritation. If you have control sometimes, then other people may be a catalyst that stimulates your irritation, but you have the ability to control it.

Negative reactions can ignite in such a short space of time that it's easy to assume that the reaction was out of your control. But just because you process certain considerations and invoke certain reactions or inhibitions below your level of awareness, that doesn't mean your reactions are out of your control. Your intuition, habits and survival instincts all inform decisions and choices, even those that seem to happen instantly.

> Some interesting studies were done where people changed their "instant" reactions without any awareness they were doing it. A fun study many years ago tested to see how fast people could repeat out loud a word flashed on a screen. Once their top speed was established, an occasional embarrassing word was flashed and people read it just as fast, but read it wrong. They were unconsciously changing the word to avoid embarrassing themselves by saying it out loud. Of course this meant that they read the word, subconsciously realized it was embarrassing and thought up a substitute, all within microseconds equal to their "fastest" time. They were unaware that they were still in control.

If you're going to change your reactions, you first have to admit to yourself that you do have some control and that how you react to others isn't their responsibility, even when they're truly irritating. Control of your reactions is your professional and personal obligation—one hundred percent your responsibility.

Walk away, but don't act unprofessional. This isn't easy, but like many other aspects of change, adjusting your viewpoint sets the stage for change.

Set Small, Discrete Goals

For some people, it may be very difficult to just stop being harsh, but one small, simple step that will start the process of developing a softer approach is to always say please.

It is hard to "not be irritable"—too general and vague a goal. But "never swearing" is a specific behavior you can pay attention to. Impatience is tough to catch unless you start trying to catch the tightness in your jaw (eyes, shoulders, etc.) that forecasts its arrival.

Working to not come off as a know-it-all raises the question, what are you going to do instead? You might try asking a question you don't have an answer to and then listen to the answer before you add your own thoughts. It isn't possible to never be frustrated, but it is possible to walk away or breathe yourself back to a calm state before you engage.

Initial small goals might be:

- Find a new saying that keeps you open to change—*People can always change*; *It's me not them.*
- Find a specific way to remind yourself you're trying to change—*I want to be calm when I'm frustrated*; *Professionals don't yell or swear.*
- Force yourself to take a brief time-out by making a commitment to take at least two breaths before you answer or talk when you're revved up. This gives you a chance to remember to try the new behavior.

- Set aside five minutes each day to visualize situations that trip you up and think about a new, more professional, more adult response. Practice the response by running the scenario through a few times in your head.
- Sit by yourself and picture in great detail a situation that "causes" you to get upset. Try to allow yourself to feel upset about the situation and then focus on your attention on your breathing until you feel relaxed. This teaches you to be in charge, not just a victim to your feelings.
- Keep a running weekly chart of the number of times you act unprofessionally, the number of times you quickly recover and the times you stop yourself before you get into it.

If you tend to be polite and rarely lose your cool, check in to see if you are too passive. Do you withhold your thoughts when speaking up would really be better? Do you keep employees on who need to be let go? Are you uncomfortable being direct about work that isn't meeting standards?

Use the ideas above to create ways to practice.

Identify Activities or Memories that Calm You

Savoring good memories gets your head into a relaxed, positive place where you're more likely to be able to unwind if you're upset.

If you're passionate about golf, think of the feelings you have walking the fairway after a good shot. Or if you're a walker, what attracts you to walking in your favorite place at an excellent time of day. I can get lost in the memory of spinning my bike down a newly paved country lane in the afternoon sunshine of a seventy-degree day. For some people, the smell and taste of a great cup of coffee will do it or the warm-milk smell of a child or grandchild.

With practice, savoring pleasant memories can change the intensity of negative feelings. Stress counselors use this technique to control anxiety, but it works equally well with frustration and irritability.

Once you get good at recalling pleasant memories and can more easily relax into a positive mood, you can begin to change your mood when you desire. Of course, it'll take practice like any other change, but the first steps are that simple.

This works well for anxiety, irritation, frustration, embarrassment and stress. If you're feeling good and you want to ruin your day, try it in reverse—remember a bad situation and it will probably help send you into a quick tailspin. Think about it, you just did it to yourself without the help of anyone.

A Few Other Techniques

- Get enough sleep. With a sleep deficit you get brain disturbances. Expect not only emotional upset and a hair trigger, but a decline in your ability to think, create, follow directions, coordinate and to stay awake.
- When sleep deprivation is chronic and substantial, psychiatrists are not able to tell whether you have a chronic mental illness or not. Read more in Section 17: Get the Sleep You Need.
- As much as possible, avoid people who are negative, complaining, blaming or discouraging. Like an unreasonable boss, these people will force you to work extra hard for no reward. Yes, you have responsibility for how you react to them, but if they're behavior constantly demands that you invest energy in modulating your emotions, you'll wear yourself out and function at a level significantly below your potential.
- When you can't avoid a negative person, try to schedule your interactions for times when you have the most reserve energy and patience—early morning, after lunch or a snack.

- Start projects in a timely manner so that you aren't under the gun with the final deadline. Stress, self-recriminations and failure encourage a cascade of negative emotions. Read more in Section 10 "Increase Your Productivity." (The next section)

- When you are surprised, by a task thrown back in your lap at the last minute or a driver who cuts you off on the way to work, you pump adrenaline into your system. The adrenaline makes you more likely to overreact to the next stimulation, no matter how minor. When you experience a surprise or other adrenaline-creating situation, be particularly careful to avoid tough circumstances for a while. It can take hours to get your full equilibrium back. If you're not careful, you might end up with multiple occurrences of your old negative pattern that will take you days, if not weeks, to unwind.

- If you get surprised by negative circumstances, plan more mini-breaks to recharge and relax. Five minutes of quiet can help add significant resilience.

- Don't go on a diet or quit smoking at the same time you start to rein in your reactions. Your discipline will be overtaxed and you're likely to slide back into your old rut. Take things one at a time until you understand how to manage your willpower investments.

- Did I mention practicing your reactions in your imagination so that they are more instinctive? Relax in your chair, picture what you overreact about, think of something professional to say and practice doing that, just like you would a presentation.

It's Hard to Ignore Feelings Until You Deal with Them

If you find yourself "out of your mind" about the people in your life, you may find it helpful to talk to a professional about the process of emotional repair. It is very difficult, probably impossible, to build a fundamentally new set of reactions and emotions on top of significant wounds from early in life, if the wounds still create major distress. The wounds might have been inflicted by family, lovers, death, trauma or can even be the result of brain health.

A good professional will act as a guide to move you out of stuck places and will help watch your flank when too much is coming at you. He or she will also encourage you to decide what to ignore and what to carefully look at. A trained professional can introduce you to approaches and techniques that are part of their area of expertise.

An experienced coach can help you change many things, but a good coach knows their limitations and may suggest that you seek help from a therapist to sort through emotions that are getting in the way of your changes. Though it may be worth trying to push through feelings, those little stinkers are tenacious and sneaky and are likely to show up again in unexpected or confusing ways. It's often better to approach intense feelings as you do any other area where your experience is limited—hire a professional, pay attention to what they suggest, keep trying to adapt proven ideas to fit you and your circumstances and work toward clear outcomes.

Be aware that changing from ducking emotions to dealing with them is a change like any other. Bring the ideas outlined here to that process and you will find yourself more comfortable and relaxed, as well as more prepared to implement other specific changes that will boost your professional standing and your personal productivity.

Section 9: Use the Clout of Simple Lists

One of the most powerful ways to reduce the discipline and effort needed to remember things is to write them down. Making lists saves tremendous energy over trying to remember.

If I ask you to memorize an epic poem like Homer's *The Iliad*, or all the details of a map of Yellowstone Park, you would think I was unreasonable. Yet this is what humans used to do. *The Iliad* was not a written document until centuries after it was created as oral history. And similarly, humans had to hold precise pictures of geography in their memories so that they could find their way back to that waterhole beside the cave around the corner from Old Faithful.

Books, maps, "story sticks"—pre-marked measurements on a stick used to build boats, houses, etc.—and other memory caches were the early forerunners of hard drives, flash drives and cloud files. We humans started to make exciting discoveries when we had access to more data than our brains could easily hold on their own.

Despite centuries of writing things down, our instinct is still to save the energy that documentation takes and "just remember it." In the immediate term that does save energy, but our brains have to work to keep that memory fresh minute after minute, hour after hour, and that takes continual effort. The net effect is a greater expenditure of energy.

This can be a bit like having too little RAM to hold all the open windows or tasks we're working on. Something will be dropped back onto the hard drive. Our physiological "hard drive" doesn't automatically take in everything our working memory needs to dump, so unless we invest even more energy in remembering, we will lose a certain percentage of the things we want to remember.

There is just too much to remember these days, and we regularly lose tasks in the period between hearing them and starting them. When we forget, the self-recriminations and blame we place on ourselves cause us to use another load of energy to quiet our emotions.

Simple lists save energy, which you can invest in creating or learning new habits.

To keep your list current, items need to be marked as completed when you're done with them. This is a simple but effective way to track whether you're actually using your list. When you track an activity—like using your task list—you're more likely to keep doing the activity until it's a new habit. So, mark items as completed. Track what's done and that you're using your list. You're effectively both implementing a system and getting your projects done.

Keep a List

- It's simple to keep a list. Just write down everything you need to remember. In Section 4, I suggested that one way to build self-discipline was to remember to carry a notebook. For those who took that small, easy step then, you now have a notebook in your pocket and all you have to do is pull it out when you want to remember to do something, or someone gives you something to do. Of course it's fine to use an electronic list, but many people find that the multiple clicks required to access the app or program mean they let capturing things slide and in the end things get lost. Try keeping your list one click away.
- Keep everything you need to do on one list. Trying to find the list you want, deciding which list a task goes on, switching things from one list to another, all use up the discipline/energy you need for other things. Keep all your assigned or accepted responsibilities in one place—I'll talk about a possible auxiliary list in a minute.

- You can use the notebook to keep your list.
- You can use sticky notes. Stick them all on one or two facing pages of a notebook or manila file folder.
- Or use a whiteboard as a place to capture sticky note tasks. If you use the whiteboard for other things, draw a boundary for the notes. This helps draw your eye to them and increases compliance.
- Also try electronic sticky notes or keep an electronic note or "task list" appointment open in your calendar. To make it easy to scan the list, bullet all tasks.
- It'll be helpful to review your entire list at least each evening or morning. Identify a set of tasks that you can realistically focus on for the next work day. If you're using sticky notes, move the tasks to a "daily task" page or separate whiteboard area. Or make a short "do today" list in your notebook or as a nonspecific-time appointment in your electronic calendar—use the appointment's note field.
- You'll probably add to your tasks during the day. Don't wait until you get back to your office or work area to note them down. Many items will get lost between hearing them and getting them on a list. Write them down as soon as you get them or think of them.
- If you have employees, use this system in plain sight. It will likely increase productivity across the entire team. Try saying, "Wait a second. I want to be sure I write that down on my task list." When people start seeing it often enough to kid you about it, you know you're beginning to have an effect on the team culture, and other people may begin to keep lists as well.

Make Your Tasks Easy to Start Doing

- Write down each task using the same system.

- Keep it short. Just write a brief reminder, not a "how to" description. Use enough detail, but only enough to be sure you know exactly what you're supposed to do. For example, It's easier to review and yet still understand everything you need to know, if you write, "Create agenda for Sue meeting" instead of putting in the purpose or an agenda draft.

- Make each task a discrete, separate action. Write down the next step on your task list only when you finish any action that is a prerequisite. The final piece of completing any task is to ask, "What is the next step?" When there is no next step, you can declare the project done.

- The next step is an action or task you can easily do without any problems. If something seems difficult or complex, you've probably not broken it down into a simple enough step for your circumstances and experience. Try a smaller step. "Discuss project with Don" may not be as helpful as "Find Don's phone number." "Create presentation" could sound overwhelming compared to "Outline possible topics for presentation."

- Begin your written description of each task with an action word, a verb like, "Call", "Research", "Find," or "Meet with." Verbs create action images. When there is an action suggested at the beginning of a task, there are no more decisions to make, just the action to complete.

- I credit the system described in David Allen's *Getting Things Done* system for many of these ideas. His system is powerful, but a bit overwhelming for many people to begin on their own. If you find my distillation helpful, you may want to take another step in becoming a list master by reading his articles or books. But take it slowly and when in doubt, keep things simple.

Which System Should You Use to Track Tasks?

- Don't get caught in trying to use all the possibilities of an involved, sophisticated system or choose the most comprehensive software or app just because it has lots of options. You're likely to spend too much time learning to use it only to discover that it's too demanding to keep up with. Chances are you'll start working around it and eventually just go back to trying to remember things in your head. Keep things simple at the beginning.

- Think about how you kept reminders in the past. Have you ever had a system that worked for a while? Consider starting with that approach again. Careful changes from that baseline can be made to find ways to make it easier for you.

- Simple is always better when you are getting started. Writing tasks down and then deleting or crossing them out when they're completed is a good starting place. Only substitute or add steps if doing so makes it easier for you to use the system. Beware of too many subcategories.

- Writing on sticky notes and then keeping a stack of completed notes can build satisfying visual evidence of what you've accomplished.

- Crumpling up notes or pages and throwing them away is a real reward for some people.

- Use check marks, cross-outs or whatever gives you satisfaction.

- If you report to someone, save all your task sheets as reminders for your evaluation reports of projects you've worked on.

- It's fine to use technology to create your full task list and then pull "do today" items off and place them on sticky notes or in your notebook. The only requirement for mixed media is that it works easily for you and nothing gets dropped. If occasionally things get dropped or skipped, simplify. And decide which list is your main one—the task list "of record"—the one you default to if there's confusion.

- Consider the idea attributed to Einstein: "Keep everything as simple as possible, but not any simpler."

Review Your Lists

- Lists are your extended memory, but the information they contain is a useless collection of hidden data unless you review it to decide what you're doing next.
- Set aside a specific time—or better yet multiple times—each day to scan your "to do" list or your "do today" list, if you use one.
- Also consider using a highlighter on "do today" items instead of a second list.
- Schedule time or circumstances to review your list—8:00 a.m. or before your morning meeting; 6:00 p.m. or before you go home.
- Weekly reviews are a time to look at your list to see what no longer needs to be there and to consider what may not have gotten onto the list that should be there.
- Once you get into the habit of reviewing your list, you may want to add other steps, such as scanning your calendar to see what's coming up that might need a task done ahead of time, or looking at each project you have to see if there is a task that you've left off your list. Again, David Allen's systems are good but a bit complex when you're trying to get moving.

How To Manage A Task You're Resisting

- Resistance is a signal that something isn't right. Use it as a reminder to clarify your task. You might stop and break the task down into a smaller or simpler first step–"Find Don's phone number", "Decide whether to use Excel or Word to present the report", "Create a beginning agenda for the meeting with Sheila."

It can help if you schedule a regular block of time to work on any tasks you've let slide or that you seem to be resisting. Label these appointments as "Must Do" or "Hard Tasks" in your calendar. At first try thirty minutes a few times a week. Only use the time to work on the stuff you've been resisting.

- Arrange a joint work session with a colleague or friend to work side by side on your individual projects. Be sure you're extremely clear that this is a work time to tackle tasks that are in danger of slipping, not a time to do easy things or to chat.

I've talked through list-making and list-keeping in some detail because it is a good illustration of using tools to change a specific behavior. One of the tasks you might create is to do an activity that involves changing a habit–"Exercise at 5:30", "Shop for vegetables", "Hold staff meeting."

Your calendar is another type of list. When you think of your paper or electronic calendar as a list with specific due dates, you get a clear sense of which tasks belong there. "Meet Jim at 8:00" becomes an appointment. But "Finish Report for Jim" doesn't, because even if it is due at the meeting, you will need to work on it ahead of time, often at a less specific time. Of course, if you're avoiding it, you may need to schedule a block of time in your calendar early on to "force" yourself to get started on it.

Trying to remember appointments is a waste of energy. A calendar frees up energy just like any other list. The calendar is also a perfect example of how crucial a regular review is. It does no good to have something in your calendar if you don't check it regularly.

Section 10: Increase Your Productivity

All the ways you do things at work comprise your system. Some parts of that system you've carefully designed. Other parts were probably cobbled together out of bits of old habits. Some systems will be easy to change—the location of certain digital file folders—others will be more difficult—the way you review projects and tasks.

This section doesn't cover all the changes that are possible in your workday. Rather, it should help you decide which of your work systems might be most promising to change to increase your productivity, and how you might specifically change a few of them. Since we've covered most of the major fundamentals of change, you will recognize many of these approaches.

Change takes repetition, so I'll both repeat ideas that apply and also lay out a few specific details for different situations.

Start with Small Things That Make a Big Difference

Taking too big a bite can cause you to choke! And while it may not kill you, it rarely leads to the smooth digestion of a change. (It's also true that carrying a metaphor too far can cause you to gag.)

Small changes can make a major difference, so look for those that provide leverage—where a small investment of attention can return a larger reward in time saved, help you feel more in charge or get appreciation from colleagues or your team. A small irritant is one possible sign of a system with potential leverage. You can recognize a small irritant by noticing what routinely irritates you. Rarely doing something the way you planned is also a clue that a small change might alter a number of outcomes.

Complexity Will Trip You Up

As I mentioned earlier, we avoid new approaches or stick with old habits when we have to work too hard to change. You probably resist things that are irritatingly complicated. The piles on your desk may be indicative of a filing system that is too complex, one that requires too much focus and/or time and therefore you continue to make piles. You may skip putting things on your task list because the list isn't always at your fingertips—opening it feels like one step too many, too complex.

Complexity is in the mind of the doer. If something feels too complex, it is. If you're not getting to it or finishing it, it's probably got some aspect that feels too complex. Complex doesn't mean you can't figure it out. Complex means you're less likely to get started on a step if it's multifaceted.

Does It Happen a Lot?

When you're considering where to start implementing changes in your systems, you might also think about frequency. Consider starting with those systems you encounter most often. They will give you lots of opportunities to practice and are the ones most likely to give longer-term paybacks and affect other systems.

Control of your email inbox may be a multiple-times-per-hour poke at your "I've-failed button." Tasks that show up daily present an ongoing opportunity to practice stating them clearly. If you show up a bit late for many of your scheduled appointments, you probably regularly face—or ignore—colleagues' quiet derision or irritation. Changing the way you manage appointments and time may be a good place to start.

If you lack a system of communication with your admin support person or have neglected to train them properly, your incomplete return-call messages may keep that shortcoming in your face all day.

Initially invest your time where you'll get a regular hefty payback.

Rebuild Valuable Alliances

Issues that regularly threaten your relationship with key team members—your reports or those you report to, including board members or investors—have the potential to pay major rewards, if they are addressed successfully. There is clear leverage in dealing with these relationship issues, as they have significant effects on productivity and retention. Having good relationships with team members and colleagues is also important in maximizing your own ability to thrive and reach a satisfying level of quality work.

This also is true for personal relationships. Fractures in intimate relationships cause an energy drag on your emotions—often this cost is hidden and ignored by hard driving people. Time invested here will almost always return multiples.

Pick the Right Issue to Start On

Be cautious of simply grabbing an issue to work on just because that's the one you're facing when you finally hit the wall and decided you must change. While that is certainly one way to decide, I encourage you to do a quick review to assure yourself that the change has a manageable level of complexity—not too much—and offers a reasonable chance of success.

And remember, you want to pick issues that happen with enough frequency to give you opportunities to practice. And hopefully the change will offer benefits to important relationships.

Keep Everything Simple

And you can't consider this too many times; if you want to change a system to make it more effective, look for the simplest next step. Be very cautious about any ideas that require too much deviation from your current habits. Big changes are exhilarating but often require an exhausting level of self-discipline to maintain unless they are very straightforward.

An example is the complexity of most paper and digital filing systems. We don't think of alphabetizing as complex, but it takes time. You must open the file or drawer, decide on the best tag for future retrieval, find the proper slot between "Cad" and "Ced." And in a paper system, create a large enough space to force the file into. Suddenly piling things on your desk or the floor seems easier.

An easier system might be to just file your material under the letter where you might look for it. Don't worry about details; just slip it into that letter's general section. The retrieval might be slower than when you take the time to perfectly alphabetize, but it's a whole lot faster than searching through random piles that have been building on your desk for six months or a year. And the odds are you retrieve less often then you file.

A complex system may offer advantages, but not if you don't implement it or use it. Don't get trapped into thinking that either you need to have a perfect system or it isn't worth starting. Getting stuck in the design stage is common. And creating a detailed system that gets replaced by piles within weeks is not unusual.

Start simply and keep adjusting until it's simple enough that you are actually using it. Only then consider adding any necessary complexity. Keep it simple enough you use it regularly, complex enough that it offers value.

Make It Easy to Start

Once you envision a new system, it's easy to want it to be a complete break from your past system. But this temptation can get you tangled in things that don't add value to your current work.

A client I worked with wanted to begin the switch to online record-keeping, but after five years of trying he hadn't made much progress. When we looked for the problem, I discovered that he was starting from the beginning, trying to scan paper records from his first year in business. He never got close to catching up to his present clients, so the most recent records were still being kept on paper. And periodically he got so discouraged that he let the whole project go for months at a time.

I told him to pick a small sample of his most active clients and scan their most recent records. Then work with the new system for a few months to identify the potential glitches—how easy is it to deal with issues when the new system goes down? Once he had the basics figured out and was keeping up with the sample list, he could start adding any new clients or old ones who made a current appointment or purchase.

Simple designs for record-keeping and implementation plans are the key to simple maintenance. Again, as Einstein suggested, "Everything should be as simple as possible, but not simpler." you can get too simple. But few of us need to worry about that.

Get to Work on Time

Being where you agreed to be at the time others expect you to be there is a sign of basic respect in most advanced business environments in American culture. Being on time shows that you value others' time as much as your own. And being on time increases everyone's productivity.

Knowing how you want others to see you—dependable and respectful maybe—can provide you with motivation to change. But the key to establishing a new habit is usually the specific, clear steps you take to change your behavior.

The complexity of most workday schedules places obstacles in the way of meeting many of your time commitments. Start with one regular appointment that has the potential leverage to affect other commitments. Choose one that is fully in your control and is simple—get to work on time. It's the one appointment that you have almost complete control over.

- Be Very Specific About the Time

  The first step is to firmly decide on your morning timetable. Create a timeline starting when you need to walk into work and figure backward. Determine when you need to leave the house, eat breakfast, get dressed, get in the shower, etc. All the way back to when to get out of bed. Set your alarm for that time and do not permit yourself to redecide that decision in the morning. (For more on this, be sure to read below or "Don't Redecide," page 58)

- Decide and Stick to It

  Failure waits beneath the Snooze button. The repetition of a thought "I've already decided!" holds at bay the temptation that there is in fact an opportunity to redecide and helps keep your finger off the seductive, little button.

- The entire process needs to be very deliberate:
  - Make a clear, unequivocal decision about what time to wake up. Do not pad your wakeup time with a few extra minutes to snooze. This is truly a time when if you snooze, you lose.
  - Know what you will do when the alarm goes off—*I will stand up, put on my robe and go to the bathroom.* When the alarm goes off don't re-think it. Do it!
  - Think through the likely re-decision temptations ahead of time—after the bathroom, do you sit back down on the bed? Be clear what you're going to do—*I will not sit down!*

- o Decide what you're going to say to yourself to block the notion that there is room to redecide. Your mantra needs to be clear and directive. Maybe say to yourself, *You've decided, get moving.* Practice the mantra. Practice until you're sure you can recall it easily when you're half-asleep.
  - o When the alarm goes off, act on your pre-made decision before the re-decision pressure has a chance to take hold—if you're feeling any hesitation, repeat your mantra. Get out of bed. Don't just lie there, stand up!
  - o Once up, congratulate yourself on your willpower—positive feedback is a motivator.
  - o Repeat for each schedule deadline you've set—shower, breakfast, being in the car, at your desk.
  - o Rededicate yourself to repeating the process the next morning. And the morning after that until it becomes your new habit.
- When Should You Leave for Work?

Being on time is a moving target. If there's traffic or the bus is full, you need more time than if everything goes the easiest way possible. While you may not want to get there any earlier than you need to, you don't want to be late. The trick is to think in terms of statistical possibilities—how many days you can fail.

According to researchers, just mentioning statistics is supposed to be guaranteed to shut down readers' and listeners' brains. I'll assume you can manage the notion of statistics, if I keep it simple enough to proceed without a calculator or paper.

How often do you want to be on time? If it is important to be on time one hundred days out of one hundred days—one hundred percent of the time—start very, very early. Early enough to find a route around the traffic accident, to find a cab when the bus breaks down or to walk when all else fails. In practice, one hundred percent is only strictly necessary in rare circumstances—the president wants to talk to you about a job in his administration, the once-a-week flight to Bali leaves at rush hour.

Generally, we only need to be at an appointment on time at least nineteen times out of twenty, or ninety-five percent. If your goal is to be at your desk at 8:00 a.m. ninety-five percent of the time, when do you need to leave to get to your desk on time? You'll need to estimate how often there is bad traffic, an accident, a flat tire, someone who talks to you outside the building, etc.

If it takes twenty minutes to drive to work with no rush-hour traffic and forty minutes with traffic, how many days is there traffic? If there is traffic three days a week, then you better be thinking about leaving fifty minutes early—add ten minutes to walk into the building. You'll need to find something interesting or productive to do with your time when you get there early.

My experience is, if you don't invest the time to identify all the tasks you need to do—clear the car windows in the winter, stop for gas, anticipate extended drive times, walk time, etc.—it isn't possible to change your habit of getting to work late. Once you know the parameters you're working with, you need to decide on the particular progress points you want to meet—being in the driveway by 7:10, etc.

It may help to decide that your workday starts when your alarm goes off. All of your morning activities are really a part of your workday routine. Decide what that routine will be and then don't allow yourself to redecide in the rush or sleepiness of the morning. When you have three months of successes, you can reevaluate your schedule and consider what changes don't threaten your new habit.

Get Home on Time

Leaving work on time can make a huge difference in your personal relationships and in the amount of creative energy you bring back to work the next day.

Getting out of the office on time starts with getting in on time, and the process of leaving is similar to getting to work.

- Make a clear decision about what time you want to get home and work backward to the time you need to begin to shut down your workday.
- Leave time to quickly arrange things so that you know where you are when you come back the next workday. A sticky note on a pile of papers can remind you of the next step you were ready to do, a couple of tasks placed on your task list keeps you from having to remember them. Be sure to save your electronic work.
- Check your calendar to assure yourself you're ready for the morning.
- Decide how long it will take to wrap up, get your coat, say goodnight to colleagues, and walk to your transportation.

If your home life is as important to you as you work life, then you need to decide what percentage of time you want to be home at the time you say you will and then calculate the risks to your schedule to arrive home as planned, say ninety percent of the time.

If you feel you've been productive during the day, it's easier to leave on time. It's common for my clients to put in extra time because they feel they haven't been as effective as they'd like. So pay attention to the next section, "Get the Most Out of Your Day" for suggestions to make the hours you spend at work valuable enough you feel free to go home on time.

It may be important to think through why you spend so much time at work. Is there a protective-resistance reason that leaving threatens something important? (Read more on this in Section 7 "Keep Your Resistance in Check.")

> One CFO I worked with felt that her value was appraised, in part, by her willingness to sacrifice. We began a careful analysis of whether that was accurate and what strategies she might use to project value and commitment to her colleagues using something other than excess hours, which penalized her family.
>
> Recognizing the key reason behind your resistance to acting on something that feels important will form the basis of your strategic appraisal of alternatives.
>
> The CFO decided that showing up a half hour before her scheduled start times and being very careful to meet deadlines ninety-five percent of the time while leaving by five thirty were judicious tactics to try. We placed a self-appointment in her calendar three months out to remind her to evaluate the effect of her strategy.
>
> During her trial period, she needed a way to quiet her anxiety about "sabotaging myself." She decided to keep telling herself, *I'm staying alert for signs of disapproval. This is a learning experiment.*
>
> By the way, it worked and some of her colleagues began to follow her lead. But those who didn't increase the effectiveness of their work days and those who failed to meet deadlines ninety-five percent of the time did get criticized.

Get the Most Out of Your Day

Changing how you arrange your workday can offer significant potential to increase productivity, efficiency and enjoyment. To maximize your productivity it's best to make a plan for your day.

If your habit is to take the day as it comes and only note the specific appointments you have with other people, you'll see huge benefits from developing a careful strategy to schedule some appointments with yourself for activities you need to get done.

Planning your day is really fairly easy—decide what you can or need to get done and then set up appointments in your calendar for specific times to do things that you find difficult.

Getting tough tasks underway is key. Here is a detailed review of how to handle tasks that are dragging you down, that don't get done or just sit on your task list week after week.

- Hard tasks need to be scheduled. You'll recognize tasks that are difficult because they're the ones you tend to put off. Don't be fooled into thinking that simple tasks are easy. If you're not doing them, then for some reason they're difficult for you. Set aside a specific time to start tasks you've been putting off.
- Most of us have a list of things that we let slip. Instead of trying to guess at the beginning of the week which ones are likely to fall behind or remain undone, it may make more sense to schedule a regular time to do any of the things on your "hard to do" list. When that appointment time comes, look at your list and choose a task you've been resisting or ignoring and get to work on it. If you complete one task on your list, start another one. Work for the entire scheduled time (thirty to sixty minutes) only on "hard to do" tasks or until you've completed the list.
- It might be worth scheduling a minimum of two "hard to do" appointment times with yourself—each day or week depending

on the volume of tasks you have. Then give yourself a bit of free time if you finish your list early. But beware, if you get distracted while you're relaxing, be sure to decide how much time you're taking so hours don't slip away.

- If you have a major project that will take a long time to finish, you might use your "hard to do" time to get started. Once you have good momentum you can schedule times to work on that specific project and save your "hard to do" appointment for other tasks.
- Be sure to not overschedule your day. Reserve time for breaks that help replenish your energy, creativity and self-discipline.

Take Appointments with Yourself Seriously

Most of us have a hard time respecting appointments with ourselves the way we do appointments with other people. Even people who are rarely late or quickly reschedule appointments with other people may casually skip appointments with themselves. To get better follow these steps:

- Put self-appointments in your primary calendar with specific start and end times, and with the same notations as an appointment with someone else—mark it "busy," not "tentative."
- Make a firm decision to start when you're scheduled to start and end when you're scheduled to end. Like other decisions you make around changes in your life, make a careful decision about the long-term results you're looking for and then don't redecide in the pressure of the moment.
- Casually running over on your self-appointments is investing time you didn't plan on spending. It's likely to make you more reluctant to schedule and keep future times. Lengthening an appointment is a re-decision you should make very thoughtfully. If you are charging along on a task and want to finish it up or put in additional time, interrupt yourself, consider how you need to use the rest of your day and then make a careful decision about continuing.

- If outside pressures actually force you to cancel your appointment, treat it like any other appointment. As soon as you know you won't be able to keep it, reschedule to a new time. Usually you'll know a bit ahead of time when you have a difficult scheduling situation thrust on you. Don't plan on rescheduling later, do it as soon as it's clear you can't keep your self-appointment. Note that I deliberately used the word "force." Don't easily give in to pressure to change your self-appointments. The most effective approach is to try to squeeze in your self-appointment early. Doing that will help you learn to take them seriously.
- Plan an "A" and a "B" time so that you have time reserved if your primary time has to be changed.
- Also be very careful about how you use general reminders in your calendar. These notations, which often get placed in an "all day" area, don't have specific start times and are therefore more like task lists than appointments. Since they have no scheduled time, they are notoriously un-motivating.

If you want to change your pattern of letting things slide, make clear, specific appointments and stick to them.

Start Your Day with a Routine

You might find it helpful to start your workday with a pattern of activities—things you do each morning.

Consider what activities have been most helpful in the past at getting your days off to a productive start—a strategy session with yourself or your team, reading emails, making phone calls, checking business websites, a self-appointment, exercise session, meditation session, review of your tasks and appointments for the day, etc. Schedule whatever gets you quickly started on your first block of time.

By having an initial routine planned, you eliminate the tendency to get distracted or waste your time with indecision and inertia, which can easily pull you into unimportant activities.

Schedule Unscheduled Time

Because this is so important and so overlooked, I want to underline the importance of unscheduled time. Not scheduling work blocks can lead to a waste of time. But if you do start scheduling large portions of your day, be sure to build in substantial blocks of unplanned time to react to unexpected demands. You might leave fifteen minutes at the end of most scheduled appointments or schedule a "free" thirty minutes every few hours. When you get to this unscheduled block, if there is nothing pressing to do, then you have the wonderful option of taking a quick walk or choosing some other way to recharge your energy.

Schedule Review Time

Scheduling a "weekly review" can be a powerful organizing and motivating tool. It's surprising how the act of reviewing your immediate past and future responsibilities can organize and focus your work week.

There are more complete and effective ways to structure a "weekly review," and the "Getting Things Done" system from David Allen can walk you through the benefits and details. I find that starting with a simpler approach is a good way to kick-start change.

Set aside fifteen minutes to look at appointments from the past week. See if any remind you of things you offered to do or were assigned. If so, be sure they're captured on your task or project list, or noted in your calendar. Then look at your upcoming week and plan how much time you need to prepare for any scheduled obligations. This is a good time to set start dates for projects, if you haven't done that, and to schedule "hard to do" blocks of time.

Next, scan your project list to see if you've scheduled work blocks to keep you on track to meet all project deadlines. Each project should have a next step either scheduled or on your task list.

Finally, look at your task list and see if there's anything you've completed that needs to be removed, anything you need to clarify because you've been avoiding it, anything you've decided not to do can also come off your list.

Get in the habit of reviewing your obligations. It will tend to keep you more focused on working toward outcomes for the day or week instead of just reacting to things that get pushed at you.

Set Aside Time to Plan

Another chunk of time that's worth scheduling is "planning time."

Be very deliberate about taking time to think about goals, approaches, as well as team and individual performance. Scheduling time will pay significant dividends in future outcomes. My experience is that leaders who set aside time to deliberately consider future trends and activities are more prepared to take advantage of opportunities and more able to hear the small voices that herald changes or developing issues.

A word about urgent versus important may be helpful. Too often busy, creative people respond to urgent needs and overlook important ones. Important tasks and projects are the ones that will make or break your business or leadership. Taking time to plan starts a virtuous cycle. Scheduling planning time can focus you on important issues and those issues will then become visible enough to demand you plan how to accomplish them.

Organize Your Work Space

Little changes in physical organization can snowball and offer leverage. Many people find that rearranging their work space has a positive effect on their work systems. I've already covered some of this, so I'll only give a quick review of the principles.

- Keep things in plain sight and close at hand if you want to encourage yourself to use them more regularly. A checklist bulleting the items you want to review during your "weekly review" session needs to be kept where you keep stumbling across it—on an open space on your computer desktop, on a sticky note on the cover of your task-list folder, stuck to the wall above your computer, on your desktop. You get the idea. Don't put it neatly away in your drawer, unless you constantly open that drawer. A sample checklist:
    o   Review project list for completeness
    o   Review projects on list for next tasks
    o   Review calendar for missing next appointments
    o   Make task list current
    o   Review upcoming calendar for start times and deadlines
- Assuming you use an electronic calendar, you might try putting the checklist in the note field of your recurring "weekly review" appointment. Open the appointment when it alerts you and the list is there with no searching—and always available anywhere you have the calendar.
- Place physical objects you want to remember somewhere in your path. Visual clues are amazingly effective reminders. If you're trying to get into the habit of always taking a note-capturing device to meetings, leave it next to something else you do always remember to take—such as a jacket, keys, briefcase or cell phone.

- Make it convenient to use electronic devices or paper to replace holding things in your memory. If you take notes on your tablet, get it out before the meeting starts, open it to the note program you use, then open and label the new note and place it right in front of you. If there is any chance the other participants think you might be texting, or are otherwise distracted, let them know that you will be taking electronic notes.
- Use boxes and baskets instead of piles. Containers create visual limits that alert you it's time to cull the accumulated mass of things inside them. They also keep the stacks from cascading onto each other.
- Also consider horizontal piles instead of vertical ones. Place all your bills in a hanging folder—you don't need to organize them, just capture them.

Remember, keep it simple.

Start and Finish Projects on Time

Set clear start dates. Most of us focus on the end date or deadline as the date we need to put in our calendar and pay attention to, but of course, that means we are preparing to run right into the limit of time we have available. The crucial date you need to schedule is the start date. When do you need to get started so that you can manage the project in the most relaxed, creative, and highest-quality manner necessary?

Many people can't feel the urgency of a deadline until it's imminent and even then it helps if an outside authority figure pressures them. When you're the one in charge, you need a better system. Setting a firm start date can help to create a heightened sense of urgency with sufficient time—hours, days or weeks ahead of the deadline.

Here are some ideas about how to get a project off to an early, good start:

- When you receive an assignment or decide to take responsibility for a project, within one or two days set aside an hour to organize your first steps.
    - Start a page of "Project Notes" where you identify:
        - The outcome you want to achieve—the product, service or project and its impact; the report and its effect on stakeholders; the process and its impact on the team, etc.
        - The due date—create one, even if it's somewhat arbitrary
        - Major milestones to alert you to check in on progress and the risks affecting probability of completing the project on time and with the quality you need
        - A rough timeline that works backward to a conservative, firm start date
        - Risks you may need to mitigate in order to meet your goals or deadline. These can be steps that you're likely to resist or need to learn, resources that you don't yet have, distractions that may interrupt your progress, etc.
    - Write a rough outline of the report, set up a planning meeting with the team, list the people who need to be involved, know appropriate contractors or vendors, create the initial spreadsheet, draft the job description, etc.
- Schedule time for your first dedicated work session. Give yourself at least an hour and then enough additional time to review your "Project Notes" to see if you need to modify any of your assumptions or plans.
- Describe a specific next step for any area of the project you're likely to resist, don't understand or need additional help with.
- Set regular scheduled work times devoted to the project, beginning on your start date. Also set regular reviews of your timeline to be sure it remains reasonable.

Most of the problems with getting projects done on time are getting them started with enough time to complete them and knowing what difficulties you're likely to run into. Getting a couple of quick work sessions in right away both gives you a bit of momentum and helps clarify what issues you may run into. You can get started without additional immediate decisions.

Say No to New Projects and Responsibilities

Your best plans will fall short if you don't know how or when to say no. Don't let your enthusiasm or lack of time to think, influence you to say yes when you need to say no. This is a change you'll probably need to slow down and think through and practice.

Some interesting research shows that on first impulse we tend not to judge our own abilities very well—this may include the ability to know what you can accomplish in a given amount of time. We usually overrate but occasionally underrate our abilities, and it's only after a moment's reflection, during which our brains get a chance to bring their full capabilities to the evaluation, that we can estimate our skills or the time needed more accurately.

When people are asked for self-evaluations, they often give unrealistic answers about their abilities. But if they are allowed to pause for that moment and are again asked the same questions, their answers are a more realistic assessment.

"How good are you at estimating time?"

"Excellent."

Pause. "How good are you at estimating time?"

"Oh, pretty good when I'm paying attention. I mean I'm okay."

This information may be particularly important for those who have a tendency toward impulsive and overly hopeful projections. Consider those times when you've quickly answered a question about when you will be home, "I'll be there in half an hour!" After pausing for a minute to consider and work out the actual undertakings involved, you might decide that the correct answer should likely be, "An hour or more."

If you develop the habit of pausing before estimating, you will give yourself time to realistically compute details and allow your intuitive side time to process relevant unconscious information and experiences. Your reliability is crucial to your reputation and long-term success, so don't answer "Sure!" without a pause to deliberate. Put the brakes on your old habit of spontaneous answers. Practice a specific reply that is both cooperative and announces that you're going to take a second to consider your answer.

"Can you take on this new project? It's due Friday."

Pause. Take a breath. Now, schedule a longer pause by saying, "Let me check my schedule and task list to be sure I give you a realistic answer." Knowing what you'd *like* to answer is not the same as giving a good answer under pressure.

You've practiced saying yes for years, so that's what you're likely to say unless you practice a new response, "Let me check my schedule and task list to be sure I give you a realistic answer." Try it a few more times. You're trying to get your mouth to form the words before you even think—that's what practice is good for. This may be a time to visualize yourself in a situation, answering the new way.

If you feel pressure to answer yes to the person asking you to take on a project, be transparent. Walk them through your task and project lists— another great reason to have a comprehensive list. Ask them to consider with you what project might be pushed back. Don't let them off the hook by agreeing to take on the project while assuming you'll figure it out by yourself later. It helps them to know that you're busy enough you'll need to juggle things.

An old trick used by salespeople can be helpful here. When you ask for thoughts on reprioritizing your tasks, wait for the answer no matter how long it takes. If they're faced with your silent waiting, the other person, whether a report or boss, is more likely to decide to try another solution—another person, or suggest which task to set on the back burner for a short time.

Say, "These three projects are on my ASAP list. Is there one we can put off until this new one is complete?" Now wait… Waiting is hard. You'll feel pressure. You may want to fill the silence with a capitulation on your part. Block any anxious utterance by saying to yourself, "Breathe and wait…breathe and wait…"

Again, it is important to remember that what you're negotiating is your reputation for reliability. Don't let someone else's agenda harm your reputation.

While it may be important not to say yes, it's also helpful to realize you're not saying no. You're asking good, reasonable questions, which you don't have good answers to, and you're being transparent about the issues you'll need to consider. This should help the other person get their expectations in order and not come back later surprised at a missed deadline or slow response.

Section 11: **Start Saying What Needs to be Said**

If you were raised on the notion that you should "play nice" with others, be a good little girl or boy, be the kind of person others will like or all of the above, it's probably difficult to say things that might upset someone. If you usually end up feeling uncomfortable when you tell someone something that upsets them, you'll tend to avoid expressing your ideas or feelings in a straightforward manner.

Is It Confronting or Conversing?

For many people it is difficult to "confront" other people, so they avoid tough conversations. Because the words you choose affect your thinking and therefore your actions, it's worth looking at the word "confront" and how it might affect you.

When we disagree with someone about an issue or their actions, we may automatically think of that as a "confrontation." And it can easily become just that. One dictionary definition of confrontation is "a face-to-face meeting or encounter, especially a challenging or hostile one." Another is "conflict between ideas, beliefs or opinions, or between the people who hold them."

If we see a conversation as hostile, challenging or a conflict, chances are we will carry at least a bit of that attitude into that conversation and inadvertently invite some of the same back. A question to ask yourself is, do you want a confrontation or something else. I'd suggest that a "conversation" captures more of the notion of what most of us would ideally like—an exchange of ideas or an attempt to understand each other's point of view.

If you change to this more positive premise, your preparation and delivery is likely to be very different than when you prepare for a confrontation. If understanding is the goal, even difficult tangles have the potential of ending up with shared good feelings, or at least not hostility.

Don't Surprise People

If you need to have a conversation about an issue or disagreement which will eventually be resolved by you deciding what approach to take, be very clear with them that you will be making the final decision. You may not be used to declaring your intentions about your decision-making process up front, but doing so will often short-circuit a misunderstanding during the resolution phase of a conversation. (I talk more about decision making in Section 12 "Making Better Decisions.")

The conversation to be more difficult if you force the other person to deal with the added element of surprise. If you're not the one who will make the final decision, ask the person who has the power to decide, how the decision will be made—so that you don't have to cope with your own surprise.

Don't Try to Get Agreement Too Soon

In prepping for the conversation—e.g., about different ways to move forward or what to do about inadequate performance—consider what outcome you're looking for. You may think it would be ideal if the other person quickly changed their mind and agreed with you. They however, will likely have a similar goal for you, and pursuing those differing ends risks stimulating resistance from both of you and encouraging each of you to dig in your heels.

Don't start a difficult conversation with the goal of quickly coming to an agreement. If you do, you will likely slip into a win/lose debate. If you want or need to have an ongoing personal or professional relationship with your conversational partner, you must place a higher value on maintaining or even enhancing the relationship. This may feel time consuming and unnecessary but it is an investment in future productivity and efficiency that has huge bottom-line potential.

The interplay of divergent ideas is the cornerstone of resilience and creativity in business settings. By welcoming disagreements with more cooperation and fewer arguments, you're encouraging everyone to speak up, both to express an opposing opinion and to alert you that a confirmation bias—seeing only evidence that supports your viewpoint or interpreting all data as supportive of your viewpoint—is imbedded in yours or the group's opinion or perception.

First Understand, Then Resolve

You need to plan for two or three conversation stages.

The goal for the initial stage is to become thoroughly familiar with each other's point of view, thinking and intuition. To gather this data, ask questions about anything you aren't positive you understand and ask for confirmation that you're correct on anything you think you do understand.

Keep asking your conversational partner "Is there anything you think I may not fully understand yet?" If you feel impatient to move on, ask yourself, *Am I positive they would agree that my explanations of their ideas and concerns are accurate?* and *Do I feel well enough understood that I would be comfortable having them explain my ideas and concerns to someone who disagrees with me?*

The goal is to be absolutely certain that you fully understand each other. This stage is like research—very different than debate. You're gathering data in order to come to the best decision. You're not looking for arguments that confirm your starting bias. The only way you will both adequately complete the "understanding" step is to avoid anything that makes you or the other person feel you have to defend your position.

Before you try a new approach, it's important that you plan and practice your part of the conversation. It may be customary for you to just start talking and adjust what you say as you see the other person's reactions. But if you really want the person you're talking with to hear what you have to say, you need to help them avoid becoming hostile or defensive. People can't listen well when they don't feel safe. Hostility or defensiveness is the result of not feeling safe.

It is crucial for your understanding of the other person's position that you help them feel safe, especially if they disagree with you or are sure you don't understand them. If they don't feel safe, they may withhold important information, which will leave you inadequately prepared to make the best decisions. It's also important that they maintain an approach to the conversation that helps you feel safe and that encourages them to understand you. If they don't feel safe, they're unlikely to treat you in a way that creates safety for you.

To create safety it's better not to take an absolute stance—as if you know best. You need to be equivocal in your statements and questions—*I have a different impression of what happened.* You need to remain open-minded. Our brains and our culture have fooled us into thinking that we know the truth when the best we know is our one-sided understanding as seen from within our own mind. We also only have part of the facts—not the facts as the other person or people know them. And we all run what we experience through a filter that is biased toward expecting our past experiences will probably be repeated.

Eye witnesses are most often wrong about important facts. If you're sure that you're right, beware. Research suggests that the surer you feel the more likely you are to be mistaken. Those who do the best job predicting the future are the people who are continually looking for new data and who remain very open to learning that they may be wrong. Everyone miss-sees, misjudges, misunderstands and misinterprets regularly. If you don't think that you do, you're misjudging the reality of your condition.

Listen Before You Leap

It's hard to have the patience to listen to someone when you're pretty sure you already know what they are going to say. If their point is obvious, and they talk slowly or keep repeating each argument a number of times, it can drive you up the wall.

In order to keep listening for the odd piece of data or emotion that might be new or offered in a way that might allow you to reach an easy agreement, you need to stay curious. Ask yourself questions—*Do I really get everything they're saying? Is it possible that I've missed a small but important piece?*

I encourage you to assume that you aren't aware of something that could impact your thinking. Assume you're missing something and then listen carefully to identify what that is. You'll never know for sure unless you listen carefully. Changes—new ideas—often first appear as the musings or opinions of odd individuals—peculiar people or only a few individuals.

If you want to be at the leading edge of new notions, listen carefully to different or unusual concepts. Some of them will flower into the new normal. Be like top business leaders or professionals, strain to hear these unassuming prophets of change who may foretell the future.

Your competition hopes that you'll not have the patience to listen through screamingly obvious comments and disconnected musings—that you'll keep interrupting your team members and miss something. Your competition hopes that you'll discourage team members from feeling valued and significant and as a consequence they'll want to change companies.

Of course some of what's said is pedestrian to the point of stumbling and not worth your time or attention. And yes, some of what people are saying deserves to be roadkill along the fast lane of business. But if you assume you know what's being said, you'll miss a lot of value. Can you afford to miss anything of worth?

- Use the time when others are talking to see if anything stimulates a new idea in you. This is called lateral thinking—see a snowball and think about how habits get compacted into shapes that are hard to break but can slowly melt. *She's suggesting we do X. Where could that lead our efforts?*
- To check out that you still understand everything, ask the speaker if you heard them correctly. Repeating their main points will force you to listen. Then ask if you have missed anything.
- Ask people to email you their thoughts. But you must read them carefully or you may as well be ignoring them when they talk to you.
- Tell your team you have a hard time listening, but that you want to hear them. Ask them to give you the bullet points first. Then repeat them back and let them tell you what you missed. They may not have been clear or you may have zoned out.
- Set aside a time each week for team members to share their ideas. Call these something like "Searching for Trends" meetings. Encourage both concerns and new ideas. Ask people to share only one at a time and go around the team. If there is time, go around again. This encourages people to prioritize.

If you want to enrich your bottom line, retain your best employees and be on the leading edge of changes, listen patiently.

Grit your teeth and pull your hair out, but listen!

Create a Safe Space for a Hard Conversation

Here are some fundamentals for having a safe, nonconfrontational conversation:

- Use words and phrases that underline that you don't know the Truth, that you only have some of the information—"This is often the case; My experience is…; From what I can see it looks like…"
- Constantly ask questions that reflect your sincere willingness to be corrected. "What am I missing? Can you think of something I haven't thought of?"
- *Do not* try to convince someone that you're right. You may be, but there's a good chance you're only partially correct, or more likely not even that much.
- Don't begin the second part of the conversation—the part where you decide what's going to happen—until you are both sure that you understand each other.
- Lay out the ground rules at the beginning of the conversation and insist that both of you stick to them. "The first thing I want is to be sure we understand each other even if we disagree. Please let me know if you feel I am missing some part of what you're saying. I don't mean whether I agree or disagree, but do I really understand what you're saying. I'll try to not make a pitch for my point of view. I want you to help me understand you before we move on. And please don't try to sell me on your point of view either. Help me understand what you think and what facts you have. Okay? I'm only interested in discussing a solution after we understand each other."
- First let the other person talk. They're more likely to listen if they've had a chance to talk. Give them lots of time to help you understand them and their point of view.
- Mostly listen and do very little talking until you understand what the other person is saying. It may help to repeat to yourself, *Listen carefully.* Or *Stop thinking of rebuttals and just listen for a while.*
- Think about what assumptions you're making and try to ask truly curious questions. "I'd like to understand better. Please share some of the information that helped you arrive at this

conclusion." It can work even in extreme cases such as, "Help me understand why you think it's safe to have you drinking at work?"

Once you're fairly certain you understand each other, you need to move to the resolution conversation. Are you the one who is now going to decide? If so, let the other person know up front (see the next section, "Make Better Decisions"). If you're going to make a decision together, then ask the other person to help you figure out what you can do to reach an agreement that addresses all the issues you both have.

> "How about if we take a few days to get more information about X, then we'll have a better idea which way to get started. This is going to be a learning process, so we need to be sure to continue to assess new information."

If you continue to ask questions about proposals that don't initially appear applicable, if you listen more than you speak and maintain an open-minded attitude, the steps you take toward a resolution are less likely to be viewed as a win/lose approach. It's pretty surprising how often just listening well to each other and keeping your shared goals and concerns in mind will allow an easy resolution to occur.

You may not ever enjoy tackling difficult conversations, but you are much less likely to go through the endless struggles and stress involved in avoiding them if you decide to change from confronting to understanding and resolving.

Be Transparent

Many people feel that being careful and evasive is polite. It isn't. It's confusing and often leaves both people feeling perplexed and guarded.

You don't have to be rude to present your feelings and thinking in a straightforward way. You need to share your feelings, not act like you know the truth. Some examples of transparency follow.

- "I can't follow your thinking." Avoid—"Your thinking makes no sense." Why—The only thing you know for certain is how the thinking appears to you.
- "I feel disrespected." Avoid—"You're being disrespectful." Why—If the person doesn't feel disrespectful, the conversation switches to whether you're right or wrong, not whether you *feel* disrespected.
- "When it sounds like you're telling me I'm wrong I get defensive; I want to hear you, not be told I'm wrong." Avoid—silence. Why—You need to create a work environment that works well for you and other reasonable people. Insist without blaming.
- "I'm feeling doubts that you have a workable plan to change your behavior. I haven't seen any evidence you're making enough progress." Avoid—"You can't change; nothing's changed." Why—Are you trying to argue there's been no change in their eyes, or there hasn't been enough to satisfy your requirements.

Transparency means revealing to the other person what's going on for you—revealing without blame, disrespect or acting like you are the arbiter of truth. Transparency often feels risky in environments where other people are playing political games. Or where you're trying to move from evasive strategies to a straightforward approach. Being open isn't always the best approach, but it is more often than most people assume.

It's ironic that vulnerable is often the strongest position to hold. If you've shared your vulnerability, it's harder to use it against you. You're the one who set the stage and wrote the script. You've become the trustworthy one. You're daring others to have the courage to join you. It's not always a winning strategy, but it's amazing how often it breaks up a confrontation and creates cooperation.

I once fired an administrative assistant who was unable to adjust to the office's demand for consistent quality. I was transparent about my discomfort and my inability to find a way to help him. "I've tried a number of times to explain what you had to change. Apparently I haven't been able to make the problem clear for you or it isn't something you are able to change. I'm sorry for that. I like you and wish it had worked out." He stayed in the organization and when he saw me in the hallways he introduced me as the best boss he'd ever had.

The first step in moving to transparency is to identify what's going on for you. Then practice words that explain without making anyone else wrong or responsible for your feelings or actions. A first step might be to let the person know that you will try to be transparent.

You don't have to share everything you think or feel. In fact, don't share everything! This isn't therapy. This is being more genuine and respectful. This is allowing other people to see the process you use to decide issues or to control your impulse to confront or blame.

Each of these steps opens the door for you to increase your open communication and encourage your communication partners to do likewise.

Section 12: **Make Better Decisions**

Decisions often lead to change and disruption. Some teams become unsettled every time a major decision is needed. Decisions are like billboards announcing who has power, whose opinion matters and whether non-leaders are included in what's going on. If you're having trouble making decisions or selling decisions to your team without creating resentment, here are a few tips:

- Experts don't try to make perfect decisions, especially when time is critical. Look for a good decision and get started, then adjust as you go. Occasionally an exploratory decision will cost you extra time or energy, but often you'll end up with a better course of action and will also save time with this design-build approach.

- Experts tend to compare a current need for a decision to past situations that were similar. They intuitively consult their "experiential templates" and look for good options they've experienced in the past.

- Decisions are significantly weighted toward your intuitive or emotional preferences. You and your clients, and almost all humans, will tend to make decisions based on an emotional preference and then look to justify or disqualify that decision with data: "I like the blue car. Let's see, it gets thirty-five miles per gallon and has an excellent reliability record. I'll buy it!"

- Old-fashioned training in how to make decisions says that you need to compare a decision to a tree of options or to a checklist of possibilities. This only works with very simple decisions, ones with only a few variables. Complex decisions—many variables—depend on intuition and past experience.

- Collect as much information as you can get your hands on with moderate effort. Then make your best decision based on the facts you have. The decision will be pretty clear, if not, the choices may be too close (see below) or you need to find an expert who has some practical experience you don't yet have.

- If you're having trouble making a decision between two choices, then chances are the options are both okay. The closer the options, the harder the decision until at some point you are likely to lock up with indecision. The odds say that a coin flip will be as good as anything and much better than inaction.
- When you're stuck, make practice decisions. Choose a path and see what it feels like to live with that choice. These practice decisions give you time to think through variables, pay attention to your feelings and get comfortable with the notion that there are very few perfect decisions.

Minimize Blowback

The way you make a decision can stimulate group tension and dissatisfaction in unexpected ways. You can avoid a lot of grief if you avoid surprises. Before you start the process of moving toward a decision that will affect your team, set their expectations. Decide who will make the decision and how. If you're going to ask for initial input, be sure you tell them how the eventual decision will be made.

Knowing upfront what the process will be eliminates mistaken expectations and surprises, which usually trigger irritation at you.

Four Major Forms of Decision-Making

1. **My Way—"I've made the decision."**
   With this approach, the buck stops with you. You feel you have all the information you need and accept responsibility for how the decision turns out. You can't see how additional perspectives will add anything. You might use this when there is a need for immediate action.

2. **Consult with Team—"I'll make this decision, but I'd like your thinking."**
    The input of others is valued, but you may have concerns the team doesn't know about or may not be able to weigh accurately. This decision may be important to the future of the business or to creating a business that reflects your personal style. You alone will be responsible for how the decision turns out, but you feel others may have ideas that will help you make a better decision and they would feel good about having input.

3. **Majority Rules—"We'll take a vote to decide how to proceed."**
    You'll do what the majority decides. After listening to all the ideas, everyone will vote on what approach to take. You feel that the "wisdom" of crowds will point in the best direction. Or this is a fairly unimportant decision and it would do the team some good to decide.

4. **Consensus—"We'll make this decision as a team and will only proceed when we all agree."**
    Everyone gets to fully participate and the final decision needs to be embraced by everyone. This approach takes as much time as it takes—often quite long—and it can bring up periods of disagreement and stress, but tends to build team cohesion.

Choose the way the decision will be made and then declare it up front so everyone is clear about the process, stick to what you say you'll do and don't bemoan the process later—it was your choice to make the decision that way. If it didn't work as well as you'd hoped, it's an opportunity for you to learn. You can tweak the process next time.

How to "Sell" Your Team on a New Idea

Again and again, clients tell me about hearing an idea at a conference or a staff-training idea from me that they want to share with their team. At the next team meeting they present the idea with lots of enthusiasm.

They talk about how it works and why it will be a great addition to the office procedures. But the idea barely makes it out of the room alive, and if it does, it often quickly gets locked in some mysterious idea-closet and dies from neglect.

Ideas aren't worth the breath you use to explain them, if you can't implement them with your team. Here are some dos and don'ts to help you sell any valuable idea. Oh yeah, that's the catch. The ideas have to have merit, or solid-gold bars won't convince your team to do more than prove the idea is worthless.

- Ask questions to elicit whether your team sees the same problems or possibilities you do. And no fair asking questions unless you are truly curious about team members' real impressions. Asking questions and then pouncing with an argument to show that their thinking is misinformed is a prescription for failure.
- Appeal to the personal desires and visions of your team. These are different from the vision you created for the business or practice. What accomplishment sparks the interest of members of your team? This is where you'll find the motivation for change. You discover these by asking insightful, truly curious questions.
- Try to show how your present system already incorporates some aspects of the new idea. Show your team they aren't starting from scratch but building on current successes.
- Acknowledge every effort to adopt the new idea. Criticizing failures is a dead-end road. Acknowledging partial successes is a powerful way to influence additional efforts.
- Follow up, follow up, follow up! If you don't keep reminding, trying and expecting, you won't get your team to follow through.

Section 13: **Encourage People to Tell You the Truth**

Changes occur because new ideas and possibilities suggest opportunities that go beyond where you are today. Most of these possibilities start as very small, quiet voices whispering in someone's head. If you want to be sure you get to hear about those quiet ideas, you need to do more than allow team members to share what they hear. You need to encourage—even beseech them—to speak up.

Your team is unlikely to share all they see and know unless you make a major effort to create a safe environment for them to talk about things you don't necessarily want to hear about. This is a major change in the way most leaders relate to their teams. As a consequence, team members practice the age-old organizational tradition of not risking the goodwill they've carefully built up by speaking their view of the truth to those with more power—you.

Leaders, managers, bosses and supervisors all hold the power to withhold rewards and fire employees. Rewards include assignment to good projects, good evaluations, smiles, general trust and responsibility. If you have that power, you can't fool people into thinking you don't. You can't act like you've abdicated your power when you haven't genuinely done so. You won't fool anyone with contrived declarations like "We're all in this together." If you have power, you must accept it and you must assume that few, if any, will ignore it. You can be a nice person, but that doesn't change the fact that you have the power.

To change the way your team members protect themselves and you from negative information or differences of opinion, you will need to say and demonstrate your willingness and desire to hear what others say.

- Never critique someone for sharing an opinion. You don't have to follow their advice or idea, but you must make them feel welcome to share more ideas. "Thanks for suggesting that. Let's keep an eye on it and see how it might work." "I really appreciate that you took a risk to suggest something so different. We need to consider lots of ideas if we're going to find creative ways to do this." To change your response, you may need to take a small breath before you respond. Try always saying, "Thanks for the idea" as a way of stalling to allow your thinking to get the upper hand over any negative emotional reactions.

- Be particularly clear that you want to hear alerts and possible risks that might be developing. Encourage the alert without necessarily endorsing any proposed action. "We really need to acknowledge and monitor these kinds of small risks to be sure we aren't blindsided. Thanks for letting me know."

- Repeat your desire to have people speak up. "The potential risks to this project will probably come from some small disruption that we're likely to ignore. Please point out things you think might jeopardize our work. We don't need disruption for disruption's sake, but we do need to stay alert."

- People may eventually start trying to prove you're not walking the walk. This is a great step forward. It shows people are hearing you and testing your veracity. Use your team members' skepticism to prove your trustworthiness. You want them to feel that they've tried to prove you wrong or insincere and so far they can't.

- You'll make mistakes and say and do things that shut down the discussion. And when you do, team members will feel like it's safer to stay quiet. It's important to quickly admit your mistakes—quick admissions are more powerful than delayed ones. Apologize, explain what you wish you'd done and formally appreciate the effort that was made to keep you informed. "I blew that one, didn't I? Let me try again to say what I really want.

Thank you for bringing this concern to my attention. I value this kind of honest input and I'll try to show that better in the future. I'll make a real effort not to let my defensiveness get in the way."

- If someone confronts you with your resistance to hearing an idea or a concern, heap praise on them for their courage. Try to find some infraction to cop to—even a minor one will do. Over-apologizing for a misstep is a huge signal to your team that you are serious. Defending your action—even if you can justify it—is a mistake. "I can certainly see that my actions made you feel like I didn't want to hear your concern. That's a serious issue to me. I always want you to alert me to risks, even small ones. I'm sorry about my reaction and I will work to be sure it both *is* safe and *feels* safe to approach me. Please keep letting me know when it doesn't feel safe."

- Your team is not likely to be aware that they're "protecting" you from negative truths. They need to have their awareness honed. Remind them often that you want to hear the whole truth. Encourage them to remind each other and to stand together against any intolerance you show.

This is all easy to say, but hard to do. You're human, you'll tend to react first with an explanation or defense of your actions or position. Perhaps the most valuable advice I can give you is to admit and apologize first and only occasionally—and much later—explain. Your reaction shouldn't be about data. The other person will react first to your attitude about the relationship. Second, third and fourth they'll react to any clues they get about your attitude about the relationship. Data is just data, a part of a different conversation, which can only get successfully resolved when respect, curiosity and value are present and felt.

Another way to become sensitized to the phenomena of your own defensive reactions is to listen carefully to how other people's reactions make *you* feel. If they stimulate you to counter-explain, if they fuel your irritation or leave you feeling not listened to, if they sound insincere or almost any other negative feeling, most likely the response was defensive or one of defensiveness's little brothers—explanations.

Respond to Mistakes

When someone else makes an honest mistake, you need to be very clear that immediately sharing it with you brings no negative consequences. If you want creative, self-reliant team members, your people must not be just allowed, but encouraged to risk making mistakes.

Mistakes can gum up a team member's ability to initiate, innovate or act independently. Blame or strong criticism is the wrong approach when you want to encourage a team member to be self-reliant. Firm insistence is appropriate to correct a continuing problem.

What should you do when one of your team makes a mistake? Here are a few simple steps to guide you in handling other people's mistakes—and some criteria to judge your own mistakes and corrective actions against.

To respond to a mistake, you need a standard to evaluate the mistake against—something you and your team can use for guidance. Was the action creative, but potentially risky—an innovative mistake? Was the risk in keeping within the limits of the person's responsibility? Did it avoid pushing the bounds of acceptable threat to a client's interests, a project's viability or the business's health? If it was an innovative risk, your response should be encouraging and reflective.

Innovative mistakes are a completely different phenomenon than repetitive mistakes, training mistakes or careless mistakes. The former are to be encouraged and the latter group analyzed and eliminated. Underpinning all is the question of risk. Here is some basic information on each.

- **Innovative mistakes**—sometimes called "hustle mistakes" or "forward leaning mistakes"—are evidence that your team is taking responsibility and motivated to improve things. Once

131

you express your appreciation for their effort, suggest they share what they've learned from the experience and what, if anything, they would do differently next time.

> "That was an interesting try you made. I like the fact you took the chance to improve things. I'd be interested in what you learned and how you'd suggest others do it differently, if a similar situation comes up again."

- **Training mistakes**—or more accurately "lack of training mistakes"—reveal that the team or person is willing to try something new and simply hasn't been trained or had enough experience. It's a plus that they aren't so worried they feel they should sit on their hands. If the risk was minor, appreciation for the effort is the first step. Then ask questions about what was learned, how their training might be augmented, and whether they understand when to ask questions.

> "I like the fact you tried something based on your experience. This is an area where we should have trained you, so let's get that set up so you're ready next time. I'm curious, what did you learn from this situation?"

- **Careless and repetitive mistakes** should invoke questions that challenge the person to consider how their systems or approach failed them. These events demand a tactical plan to dramatically lower the odds that a similar mistake will happen in the future.

> "We've been through this before, and I was sure you understood what you needed to pay attention to. Would you agree that you weren't paying attention? Please tell me exactly what you're going to do so this doesn't ever happen again."

In all cases of mistakes, a key question is whether the underlying risk, which the mistake exposed the business to, was an acceptable one. Team members must be concerned about the level of gamble they are subjecting the company to. Caution needs to increase as the risk rises.

In these cases you might say, "The effort you made didn't work but I appreciate that you tried. It's important that you always consider the risk when you try something new. I think that this risk was pretty big and I'd like to be sure you understand why."

Teaching your team what kinds of mistakes are acceptable and which aren't will help raise their awareness about the costs and benefits of mistakes. Remember to have the same kind of talk with yourself when you make a mistake. Beating yourself up isn't a productive response. The effective response is to look at your system and discover what caused the mistake or what might prevent it.

If changing your behavior feels like it demands significant adjustments of your attitude:

- See Section 8, "Tempering Your Emotional Reaction".
- Practice what you want your specific reactions to be when you're challenged or someone makes an honest mistake. Write initial responses to specific circumstances and practice saying them until your mouth does it without you having to direct it.

Section 14: **Change Who You Hire**

If you're only hiring people who act or think like you do, then you may be risking your business.

Resilience comes from having a diverse set of eyes watching out for both changes and new ideas worth exploring. Businesses thrive when they keep learning and growing. There aren't many better ways to bring growth to an enterprise than to bring interesting people together to bounce ideas off each other.

To get out of the rut of hiring the same type of person, consider these steps:

- Think carefully about what your current team doesn't have. Often it's someone who is constructively pushy or who is slightly irritating in that they champion ideas that aren't the ones you and other team members see as obvious.
- Employees of different social, cultural, age, gender, sexual orientation, race identification or regional backgrounds aren't guaranteed to bring different ideas, but they should be interviewed carefully in the hopes they might spice up your team with new viewpoints—just living with any of the above perspectives creates alternative viewpoints.
- When you interview, ask for examples of how candidates think about a number of issues that might be important to you. Of course you want them to have basic traits like integrity, ethics, persistent effort, etc., but you also want to see if you can sniff out nonlinear thinking—can they see odd connections between various ideas, e.g., new services you might offer and something totally disconnected such as historical trends in music? You might ask them to give you some examples of ideas they think are

interesting, that in the past they haven't gotten much agreement on.

- Ask team members to interview candidates and pay close attention to concerns they raise. Try to dig deep to discover the real reasons behind comments like, "I don't think they'd fit in with the team", "They don't seem to have the same idea about things as we have." Again, it's not that the concerns aren't legitimate, but when others have vague, rather than specific, concerns there's a possibility you're looking at a candidate with a valuable alternative perspective.

- Encourage candidates to question your team about an area that will be included in their responsibilities and then ask them to throw out some wild ideas about possible ways of doing things. Tell them you're looking for silly ideas, which most likely aren't implementable. Keep it all theoretical and lighthearted so they share ideas without worrying about what they don't know.

- If you hire someone who has different ideas, you certainly don't have to agree with them, but hopefully you will pause and welcome their creativity before you reflexively decide whether or not to explore their idea further.

You'll probably have to keep reminding yourself that people who feel slightly irritating to you may be a catalyst that can help you create a breakout service, product or approach to clients and customers. Hire for different perspectives and then encourage team members who take acceptable risks.

Again, you need to confirm all the traditional attributes you usually look for in good candidates, but shake things up so you don't end up with a team that's lacking breadth and vision.

Section 15: **Change How You Use Electronics**

There are many habits we repeat mindlessly. After all, habits free up our brains. Some of those habits will begrudgingly step aside when we begin to build more satisfying alternatives. But others will fight viciously for their survival, if we threaten to interrupt their routine.

Many of my clients make it clear that I best not even casually question their habits around electronic distractions. If I suggest we should question the way TVs, online browsing, texts, emails and games are managed by them or society in general—or even the way cell phones are used in meetings—I'd better be prepared for a knockdown-drag-out-fight. Clients may have declared their desire to "Be more productive!", "Take charge of my work!", or "Finish projects on time!" But if I hint that they might want to question the disruptive role of their beloved electronic tools or devices, I come face-to-face with a level of resistance that the Terminator would be proud of.

Unregulated emails, access to the internet, the easy availability of video games, unregulated receiving and sending of texts and calls and even the very presence of a cell phone are all likely to be serious causes of lower productivity in the work place. Additionally, passive watching of electronic media is a known and important contributor to excess weight gain, low exercise compliance and sleep deprivation.

Electronics are Ubiquitous, but Not Innocuous

Humans are apparently poor at multitasking. If you think you are the one person who can, you are likely as deluded as a smoker who says that smoking hasn't been proven to harm health. *You can* do two things in quick succession, and *you can* repeat that loop again and again. But if you think that your performance on each and every task isn't seriously degraded—below par, less effective, inferior, lacking some degree of quality—you need to start exploring research that uses real scientific techniques, not subjective impressions.

One distressing, initial finding is that those who think they're better at multitasking are often worse than average. If you strongly disagree, ask yourself what level of productivity you're comparing yourself to. If you're distracted by multitasking, how would you know the degree of that distraction? It wouldn't be good to discover the truth through an accident that injured you or an innocent other person. Nor would it be good to spend months or years of your work life working at lower efficiency due to overconfidence in your abilities or performance, or remaining blind to how you confirm your biases—remember, confirmation bias means using all the available evidence to prove your point rather than to evaluate your bias.

Electronic distractions beguile us with their offerings but stunt our performance. Social media designers are now talking about how they design their apps to capture our brains through known psychological influence techniques. Think they don't work on you? The simple truth is, when you're online, they do to a lesser or greater degree.

Electronics are so helpful and interesting that we're likely to mistake their value and assume we need to have them always available. We shouldn't throw them out, but we must learn to control our use of them. And the first step is to know that our performance when driving, thinking, creating or relating to others is seriously impaired when electronics are capturing a piece of our attention.

If you are trying to be on the leading edge of creativity, productivity or quality, you need to develop the habit of controlling electronic interruptions and their ability to distract you.

Here are some simple steps to take:

Online or On-demand

- We perceive value in those things we spend time doing. Watching screens hooks us into perceiving value above what may be real. Value in this case may be felt as entertainment, information or distraction. There is no way to accurately judge the value until you step back from the screen and see what alternatives feel like. Try a digital-entertainment-free evening, weekend day or, for the courageous or dedicated, a week-long digital vacation.

- The way you spend your non-work hours will affect how you spend your work hours. Exercise will spur hormones that support brain development and stability. Those hormones increase your capacity in the areas requiring memory, creativity or attention. Passive watching is likely to decrease both your inclination to exercise and the amount of time you feel you have for exercise. Try not turning on the digital entertainment unless you have exercised for at least twenty minutes that day. Once that's established, increase the time.

- Pre-choose the shows you'll watch this week and stick to your list to build self-discipline.

- Label your screen-entertainment time as "lost time." This is the beginning of reframing the way you think about it.

- Try asking yourself questions like, "If I were going to die next week, what would I rather be doing?" or "Does this time support or get in the way of what's really most important to me?"

- Verbal controls make it easy to just mindlessly turn on entertainment. Can you find a way to make it harder? See Section 6 "Change with Almost No Effort".

- Research shows boredom is a positive thing for children to manage. It apparently increases creativity, attention span and self-control. Find ways to bring boredom into your life—and the lives of children you care about.

Email, Texts and Other Messages

- Messages are an important aspect of business and personal life. They can't just be shut off, but they do need to be corralled into specific time blocks. Every time you interrupt yourself to read an incoming digital message your productivity slips. It will take you as much as twenty minutes to get back to full productivity.

- Try turning off alert signals and icons. Check messages on a regular schedule, but not constantly. It might help to start and end your day with a fifteen to thirty-minute email and message period. You might add one optional scan for urgent items at lunchtime. Or schedule three to ten minutes at the beginning of every hour to scan incoming email. Once your team knows your process they'll work around it. If they need you immediately, tell them how you want to be contacted—phone, in person.

- Block out several hours for uninterrupted work. During these times turn off your message alerts.

- Set a clear policy about which emails need to be responded to by your team as "Reply All". Perhaps the default for your team maybe should be that "Reply All" is rarely needed and they should have a habit of not using it. A fun way to challenge them is to send an email stating this and see how many hit "Reply All" to confirm.

- Try to reduce the time it takes to dispense with email and other business messages.

- You can probably reduce your scanning time if you keep your inbox almost empty—completely empty is good but it can take more time than it's worth to strive for absolute empty on a daily basis.

- Create digital folders for all major communicants.

- Create a folder that's a holding spot for anything you've read but aren't ready to file or delete—a "Hold" file? This eases the time it takes to make decisions and helps keep your inbox clear so that new mail is obvious.

Cell Phones

- The very presence of a cell phone has been shown to decrease attention on the task at hand—be that a meeting, conversation, etc. Again, if you think you're the exception, you're trying to evaluate yourself from inside a funhouse of mirrors. How would you know without volunteering for a study of your abilities both with and without a phone present? If your phone is constantly at hand, it's probable you're shortchanging your productivity.

- If your employees push the rules on cell-phone use at work, consider a ban on having one in your hand except in the break room. This is tough and will bring up complaints about not being trusted, but productivity is likely to climb.

- When you're trying to create content, solve a problem or decide something, put your phone where you won't hear it or feel it vibrate. This is the equivalent of silencing message alerts. If you need to be constantly available—very doubtful—arrange for someone else to hold and answer your phone and filter your calls. Most people will wait for you to be available.

- If you don't need to always be immediately available, try setting a schedule similar to the one detailed in the messaging section to give you uninterrupted time to do your best work. Of course, if you don't need to be doing your best, you can leave your phone on.

- If you prefer text messaging to voice messages, politely announce that fact. "Hello, you've reached (name). If you'd like to leave me a message, I'd appreciate it if you do it by text or email. The third choice would be a voice message. Thank you." Suffering because others don't know your preferences is not productive.

Internet

- In survey after survey the internet is reported to be a major distraction. In most offices it is a necessary tool and therefore can't be turned off.
- If the internet is a distraction for you:
    - Don't leave your browser open.
    - Delete all shortcuts that lead to entertainment and shopping sites on your computer desktop or other devices.
    - Don't have favorites or bookmarks that lead to distracting sites.
    - Download a program that blocks certain sites, or blocks sites during certain hours.
    - Make a clear commitment that you will never go to non-business sites on your business computer or smartphone during work hours. Always keep work and play separate.
    - Do not redecide the above commitment. Try saying, "Don't redecide! Just start your next task!"
    - Block any feelings of temptation with self-talk.
    - If you're an employee, when you feel tempted try saying to yourself, "I'm being paid and it would be theft of time I'm being paid for." Grossly wasting time at work is unethical.
    - If you're self-employed, try saying, "Where do I want to be next month? What will help me get there?"
    - Ask your IT person what options there are for blocking access to certain sites company wide.
    - If your projects allow it, have a separate computer for work that doesn't access the internet.
- The threat of sanctions can help everyone control their urges, just like drug testing reduces drug use.

- o Have a very clear policy that office computers are not to be used for shopping, browsing, viewing sports. Porn sights should be absolutely out of bounds. Certain non-compliance incidents should be reason for dismissal—viewing porn or hate-speech sites are examples. But such final penalties are hard to enforce when an employee offers your business value, so it helps to have an intermediate response available. Stating that any non-business use is grounds for being put on probation with consequent temporary halt of acquiring benefits (e.g., vacation time, bonuses, etc.) can be more effective—check your state regulations before implementing punitive rules.
  - o Let your employees know that your IT person will regularly and randomly check browser-history caches. Let them know that there are ways to check even if they erase the obvious history. Make it a requirement that browser histories not be deleted. State this policy at the beginning of employment.

- Consider officewide software that blocks access to certain sites or only allows access to certain sites. If you want employees or you to be able to surf the web or shop on occasion, tell them they may use their phones during breaks for that activity.

Regularly ask employees for reports on their project milestones. Knowing that they will be asked increases the likelihood that the volume of time perceived to be available to waste on personal distractions will decrease.

It's worth remembering that families who take electronic-free days report higher satisfaction and more satisfying interactions. Businesspeople who shut off the office electronic chatter report more relaxed evenings, better family relations and better concentration and creativity at work. Consider "outlawing" after-work business emails, texts, etc. Vacations without electronics are more relaxing, and the reduced stress seems to continue even when work resumes.

Section 16: **Change Jobs**

And now a few ideas about changing jobs—a huge change, which often feels out of your control. These ideas apply to both changing employment and starting a new business or career.

- Reframe any negative thoughts you have about the tough job market, your need for retraining or your low energy.
    - "These days all employment is almost the equivalent of being self-employed. I will need to take charge of keeping my professional skills at a high-value point during my entire work career. So this is a good time to start."
    - "Eighty-five percent of the people who want jobs have one."
    - "There's always a position for someone who can create value."
    - "Persistence is a highly prized trait."
- If you are currently employed or have a business, make it a top priority to put aside a significant sum of money to help ease the possible decline in income during a career, product or service transition. If you want to avoid feeling urgent financial pressure, expect that you'll need enough money to cover six months or more. Don't wait for a bonus or year-end profit distributions. Start saving a moderate amount from each paycheck. Starting now! Then add your year-end bonus.
- You'll need to find or create an opportunity. It's less likely a job will find you. You'll improve your chances of getting or creating the position you want, if you use your current situation to learn additional valuable abilities or skills. Figure out small next steps that will move you toward your goal.
    - Manage relationships with difficult people better.
    - Learn to manage your time better.

- o Upgrade your technical skills.
  - o Improve your ability to make presentations.
  - o Get additional experience selling intangibles—i.e., your value as an employee.
  - o Take a class that gives you a taste of a new career possibility.
  - o Volunteer in the field that interests you.
- Create a strategic-scenario plan for the job transition. Unless you have a specific job at a specific company in mind, you will need to set intermediate goals. These should position you to be nimble enough to take advantage of anything interesting that comes your way.
- Here are two scenarios to prepare for:
  - o If I get offered a job I'm not sure I want, I'll...
  - o If I don't get a job offer within sixty days, I'll...
- Explore what two or three changes you can pursue or skills you can learn in order to be more prepared for a new position. Is there a skill you can learn that would be valuable in most future scenarios you can imagine?
- Consider your job search as a project and create a list of subprojects with next-step tasks for each. Update your list daily or weekly.

Projects That Prep You for a Job Search

- **Strengths.** It is difficult to sell yourself if you don't know your strengths. Spend time identifying your fundamental strengths. Make a list of those that may have value for an employer—a career coach can be quite helpful with this. Create ways to explain your strengths that involve narrative. For example, rather than "I'm persistent," try "I keep on trying until I find a possible solution. It's hard to stop me once I get started." The human brain remembers these scraps of stories better than words or data.

- **Interview.** Think about what value you offer employers. Prepare answers to tough questions about your work history and hone your presentation skills. Practice phrases or sentences that you want to use in the interview. Become so familiar with the phrases that they naturally fall into the conversation when they're appropriate. Always ask yourself what outcome you want from an interview and make the outcome something you have some control over. You have little to no control over whether they eventually hire you, but you can influence how they perceive you. The most effective outcome is probably something like, "I want them to see my value in solving the problems they think they have." This will focus your questions and answers and lead them to seriously consider you for the position.

- **Research job categories** that seem to use the fundamental strengths or skills you would hope to use in a new position. "Managing highly creative people" or "Able to execute on time and on budget" could be valuable in many fields whether they are aimed toward work teams, artists or customers. Also research other companies in your field, compensation levels, online job boards, etc.

- **Resumé.** Choose a clean style and put together drafts, get feedback from experts, create variations for different positions, draft a cover letter or email, think about how you will present jobs that look less than stellar on your resumé, contact your references to let them know you are looking. More and more, you need to be sure you include searchable key words in your resumé.

- **Network.** You are most likely to be told about an open position or be asked to interview on the recommendation of someone who knows you. Cultivate relationships with highly social individuals— those who know lots of people. No need to get really close, just stay on terms that allow you to approach them with a question like, "Do you know anyone who might know someone at XYZ Corp?" Cultivate people through activities, emails, calls, meetings, support groups, social networks, LinkedIn, etc.

- **Activities to add value.** Write blog posts or articles, learn new skills, get an advanced degree, consult, volunteer at a nonprofit.
- **Personal prep.** Lose weight, exercise, get advice on interview clothes, get coaching on interpersonal effectiveness, learn to manage your emotional state. It may not be "fair" but employers notice these things and make judgments.

Schedule free time to ensure that you work at your job transition. Block out time in your calendar. If you're not working, schedule two to four hours each day for search-related tasks. Job searches are exhausting, so don't plan eight-hour days. Be certain you get away from distractions so you complete tasks on your list.

Remember to use self-talk to keep your spirits up. "This is a game of numbers. I simply need to make more contacts." "Every time I apply or talk to someone I'm more experienced and more prepared for the next interview." "There's ninety-five percent employment." (Take the unemployment figure and subtract from 100.) "I am valuable or can make myself valuable enough to get hired."

Any given step may present you with a difficulty. If you get stuck, try breaking things into smaller steps.

If you find yourself slacking off, think about the possibility that some kind of protective resistance may be in your way. (See Section 7 "Keep Your Resistance in Check"). You might be afraid of failing or getting told you are not the right person. Not trying can seem like one way to control the possibility of disappointment. This might be a time to find a support group or coach.

Section 17: **Get the Sleep You Need**

Sleep is one of the fundamental necessities of life. We often ignore its importance, but it ranks up there with food and water in sustaining life. We may live as long as thirty days without food, five to seven without water, but we may struggle with a psychotic state in as little as three days without sleep.

Serious sleep deprivation mimics mental illness. But even if you're mildly sleep deprived, it will lower your tested IQ and affect your inhibitions and judgment. Sleep deprivation is one of the top causes of serious traffic accidents. Not getting enough sleep also lowers your immune response, and experiments with mice shows it will eventually lead to death.

Not getting enough sleep presents a serious impediment to change. You need sufficient sleep in order to have the energy and focus to practice deliberate change and build new neuron pathways. And yet, in a catch-22, poor sleep habits take willpower change—to strategize, decide and follow through on the steps to improve them.

Let's say you're sleeping six or seven hours a night and you have all the tells of a sleep deficit such as periods of feeling foggy, staring into space during the day, falling asleep in a chair if you try to read a challenging book, falling asleep immediately upon getting into bed, fighting to stay awake when you're driving, etc. Unbeknownst to you, you probably really need between seven and nine hours of sleep a night. If you're sleep deprived, it's dangerous to continue to drive, make an important business decision or have personal conversations with your spouse. It's time to change.

Three Concrete Steps to Combat Sleep Deprivation

1. Getting up at the same time helps to reset your going-to-sleep time. Decide when to wake up. Set your alarm and get up at that same time

every morning, both weekdays and weekends, until you're no longer short on sleep. At that point you can sleep an extra hour on weekend days if you want.

2. Count back nine hours from the time you decided to wake-up and commit yourself to turning off all electronic devices and getting ready for bed at that time.

3. Get into bed thirty minutes early—you can read a non-exciting book, meditate or simply go to sleep.

If you're tired and watching entertainment, it may be hard to get up and go to bed. This is another one of those situations where you need to commit to not redecide. You've decided what time to get ready for bed, so talk yourself into standing up and getting into bed. Sleep deprivation disables you so effectively that you'll be a poor judge of your capabilities and will make "sleep-stupid" mistakes—like falling asleep at the wheel, launching a space shuttle in the cold, running an oil tanker aground in Alaska, or watching another TV program.

If you don't fall asleep easily, teach yourself how. Get training in full-body relaxation techniques, write in a journal to empty your mind well before bedtime, *do not watch screens* in your bedroom, keep the lights low in the evening and get up at the time you decided even if you're still tired. If these ideas fail, see a sleep specialist. Don't start with medicine. Behavioral practices are proven to be more effective than drugs.

Sleep is a leverage change. Adequate sleep will make it easier to regulate your emotions, to invoke your willpower, to remember to use new patterns, to think of new ways to approach problems, to manage your resistance and more.

Establish a Routine

A regular bedtime routine that takes you from awake to asleep is a powerful habit to practice. Practice a pattern and it will become almost hypnotic as you walk through the steps—turn off the electronics, turn off the lights in the rest of the house, brush and floss, wash your hands and face with warm water, note in your "Worry Journal" all those things you want to park until tomorrow—"I will worry about this tomorrow."—set your alarm, get into bed and slowly, progressively relax every muscle from your toes to your scalp. If you're still awake, silently and slowly repeat a sleep mantra with each in and out breath, "Sleep and rest...sleep and rest" or "Relax and rest...relax and rest."

There are a couple of other things to watch out for.

- Beware of your protective resistance, which may try to convince you that you can manage electronics or action-adventure novels at night—either you're managing them well or you aren't. It's not uncommon that when I suggest to clients that they turn off their screens much earlier than they're used to, they feel as if doing that is like admitting to being out of control. Many people feel that they can manage the stimulation of media—most can't. You must turn off the TV or get off the computer when you need sleep. Recognize the seductive quality of digital entertainment and media, and turn them off.
- Caffeine too late in the day disturbs sleep—try to stop five hours before bedtime. It's hard to not have an afternoon caffeine pick-me-up if you're sleep deprived, but it will probably mess with the quantity and quality of your sleep.
- Wine, beer or other liquor may help you fall asleep more easily, but will interrupt the deep, restful sleep you need to be rejuvenated in the morning. Alcohol is a primary sleep aid—it reduces the time it takes to fall asleep and increases the amount of deep sleep in the first half of the night. But it backfires and makes you more restless and often wide awake in the early hours of the morning, when you get the deep sleep you need to heal, to strengthen your immune system and produce human-growth hormone.

Sex at night can be nice, but get to bed a bit early so that a long, languid session doesn't steal sleep time. Of course, if you're sleep-deprived, get to bed a bit early so that you don't inadvertently fall asleep and tempt your partner to kill you.

Be conscious about what you are trying to accomplish. If you want to go to sleep, decide and then don't redecide. Watch out that you don't start eating or doing something else to stay awake. Get the sleep your body craves and every other change will be easier.

Section 18: **Start an Exercise Program**

Humans were built to move. Our physical structure evolved to hunt by walking down our prey and that ability permitted us to kill and eat more nutritious and tastier animals, despite their superior short-term speed—as a long-term vegetarian I accept that meat had a role in human development. Modern life has less call for that ability—a nutritious piece of tofu can rarely escape. But we ignore our design specs at great peril to our physical, emotional and cognitive abilities and health.

Light to moderate physical activity:
- Reduces the risk of heart disease, diabetes, cancer and arthritis
- Increases your ability to do most things you want to do without difficulty
- Reduces the odds of Alzheimer's, various dementias and memory decline
- Increases the ability to learn, remember, focus, regulate attention and more
- Reduces emotional volatility—irritability, depression and mania
- Increases good feelings and satisfaction
- Is an excellent high-leverage activity to develop self-control with all the above side benefits

Research shows that easy to moderate activity brings the majority of the health benefits we need from exercise. Invest as little as twenty minutes a week and scientists can measure the benefits. In addition, less time spent sitting appears to be as important as actual activity—move, stand, walk; don't sit for too long.

I assume you know most, if not all of this. So why haven't you started moving on a regular basis? Look back at the sections on resistance and small steps for ideas. Here are some additional ideas to kick-start your program.

Tips to Starting an Exercise Program

- It may be more motivating to set an activity goal that requires you to get in better shape. I set goals for the next season's bike rides, backpacking trips, sailing events, etc. I find these much more motivating during periods of low energy. For instance, I need eight weeks to prepare if I'm going to do a reasonable job on that Century ride—100 mile ride—in June. That thought is more motivating than, *I'm going to ride three times a week to stay in shape.*

- One kind of goal is being able to do a particular activity with comfort. *I want to be able to climb the stairs without puffing. I want to be able to shoot baskets—ride bikes, go swimming, etc.— with my kids or grandkids.*

- Don't pooh-pooh a gradual start. Many of my clients resist suggestions to start slowly. I usually recommend starting with an increase in "gratuitous" steps, stair climbing and easy walks. Clients say, "That's nothing! I need to do more to feel like I've done something. Every few weeks or so I run three miles, a twenty-minute walk is nothing." Research shows that a twenty-minute walk every few days is more valuable than a run every month.

- If you find yourself not getting to the gym for your exercise, set a goal that doesn't require you to change clothes or go to a certain location—the gym, the track, the trail, etc. It's important to eliminate speed bumps, which may bring your weak inclination to get moving to a full stop. Your first goal is to get in the habit of doing something—anything. Only when that's established should you increase the frequency, intensity or difficulty it takes to get started. A walk will probably slide into your schedule without requiring too big a decision.

- For those of you who used to compete in sports but are now fairly sedentary, stop comparing yourself to the fewer than seven people out of a hundred who run regularly and the considerably fewer who exercise to increase athletic performance. Your first goal is to be in the thirty percent who are active—think walking— most days. This is the group that is getting almost all of the benefits of activity and taking few risks of injury. Once you're in the top of this group, take on an additional challenge only if it offers you satisfaction and pleasure.

- Track your exercise sessions. At first, note days you did something for at least ten to twenty minutes. When you have a solid track record of moving three days a week, increase it by a day and only count those times you did twenty minutes or more. Track your successes on a calendar, spreadsheet or smartphone app. Remember, tracking creates motivation.

- If you are ready to do an activity that requires a change of clothes, additional equipment or a different location, always keep your workout gear together and ready to go. Take no chances that collecting your gear will be a speed bump that dissuades you from starting. If your preferred workout time is first thing in the morning, lay out the gear before bed. And of course, don't redecide in the morning.

- If you can find a person or a group of people who have the same goals you have, you're more likely to start and stick to your activity. A supportive person or group isn't necessary, but can be very motivating. Don't let the search for the right situation inhibit you from starting to walk. There's a good chance that you'll find what you're looking for while you're out there being active.

There are a couple of warnings worth considering.

- Many women don't ever push themselves hard enough to increase their capacity beyond a moderate level of intensity— that's fine! Moderate gives you very solid health benefits. But you'll need to increase your intensity if you want to explore higher performance goals—those that require a bit of a push.

Never let discouragement with performance stop you from continuing your healthy base activity level.

- Many men won't take the slow, deliberate steps needed to build safely toward increased capacity. In pursuit of personal bests, they take significant risks of injury. This can seriously harm your goal of a base fitness level. Health activity is not a sprint, it is a long-distance quest. Seriously protect your healthy base level of activity.

- Your body is an amazingly adaptable organism, but it takes time to build in the adaptations needed to meet greater activity levels. Muscles take weeks to reach a higher stage of development—as muscles develop, tendons and bones grow to support the additional stresses. This is all great, but requires time. Positive adaptations continue for seven years or more of activity. Either be satisfied with a healthy activity base or plan on a few years of growth toward your performance goals. Again, do not risk your healthy base level of activity—or a disruption toward your performance goal.

If you're going to make only one change, just stand up and walk!

Section 19: **Change the Way You Eat**

A staggering number of people in modern societies are overweight or obese. I was one. I weighed thirty-five pounds more than my recommended weight. Over a period of two years I reduced my weight and now I've kept if off for over twenty years.

If you also weigh more than you want, some of the ideas I've talked about can help you begin a modest weight loss program, which just might develop into a new lifestyle. Here are some quick tips on applying change ideas to taking charge of your eating habits. Since too much and too little weight can lead to serious health problems, be sure these are appropriate to your situation and, if you have any doubts, check with your physician.

Eating fewer dense, fewer calorie-laden foods can be an elusive goal. Talk about protective resistance! Our bodies are exquisitely programed to resist efforts to reduce our fat reserves. Back when our meals needed to be found rather than just eaten, our very survival depended on those fat reserves.

Attempts to change will therefore push headlong against an ancient instinct in defense of your very survival. Knowing that your body is sending you misinformed and outdated signals may help you get a bit of a leg up on your emotions.

There are lots of books written on how to lose weight and I won't attempt to duplicate them here. But a number of scientifically backed tips and warnings are in order.

- Like exercise, this is a long-distance effort. Don't waste your willpower on short-term goals. Any quick-loss diet is an appeal to your impatience, your lack of ability to predict the future and an inherent weakness at imagining your future self—companies take advantage of these scientifically affirmed weaknesses.

- Tracking has been shown to increase the odds of success. Track your weight daily so you can get familiar with how it goes up or down after certain meals or activities. On a day-to-day basis your weight will fluctuate around a trend line that reveals slow gains or losses. Most people who are successful at controlling their weight over a long period of time weigh themselves every day and keep track of it.

- Tracking the food you eat has also been shown to increase the odds of controlling the amount and/or calories that you consume. There are good apps that will make this very easy. There are some commercial programs with support groups that let you choose between paper and online tracking.

- Be clear about why you want to lose some weight. The reasons need to be pretty compelling to you. Looks, ability to do activities more easily, health and self-image are all possible reasons.

- Be very alert to quiet pressures from your protective resistance. Some people feel more substantial when they weigh more, some have found weight an effective way of inhibiting unwanted advances, others feel that larger body parts increase their attractiveness. Some of the more interesting resistance comes when people feel that they are under less pressure to pull together other aspects of their lives because they're overweight. And the most common reason to resist? That darn ancient survival instinct that can't seem to get that we now always have plenty of food available.

- It is easiest to start with one or two small changes that require less self-discipline and then add new changes after you have stabilized the last ones.

- Try eating more foods that are full of fiber and water—less calorie dense—many vegetables and fruits fit this profile.

- Eat whole grains. Eat as little refined grains as practical—often white or enriched.

- Cut back on sweeteners.

- Have one small sweet treat a day and have it in the morning.
- Eat a smaller dinner, a larger breakfast.
- Measure portions of bulk and high-density foods. Use a measuring cup to serve yourself items that come in multiple serving containers.
- Pre-measure snack foods into small one-serving containers. Don't redecide to eat a bit more.
- Do not drink any sweetened beverage. Your body doesn't believe that they have calories and will lie to you—it will tell you you're still hungry. Skip the soda, juice, sweetened teas, etc. As an alternative, perhaps begin by watering them down 50/50. Or try a few sips when the urge hits and throw the rest away.
- Keep all snack foods out of sight. Even better, make them difficult to reach—in the pantry, behind the extra cereal boxes, etc. We're less tempted by what we can't see.
- Eat off small plates. It fools your eyes and your stomach into feeling fuller than a similar serving on a large plate.
- When you eat, do nothing else. Pay attention and savor your food.
- Change your self-talk around food. When you see junk food say, *That's not food. It's big business trying to fool me into eating.* Try saying, *I'm not hungry. I'm using food to entertain—or distract—myself.* Even if you sometimes go ahead and eat it anyway, you're less likely to eat as often or as much.
- Make any candy or snacks you have at work hard to get to. Force yourself to make a conscious decision to go get them and then carefully decide whether to eat them. The extra work will slow you down.

The book *Mindless Eating* about how to eat less without noticing has many other helpful, interesting facts and ideas.

You will slip and fall off the wagon. Plan for how you'll recover. When you notice you have stopped eating either what's good for you or the amount you should have, you might weigh yourself, start your tracking chart again, get all the snacks out of sight and simply start again. The second time around is easier than the first time.

Section 20: **Learn a New Skill; Perfect an Old One**

Learning a new skill or perfecting an old one is a change. But there are some things that need to be emphasized when you're learning a physical skill—changing the way you perform a physical action like typing, playing a musical instrument or refining a new move in your sport, dance or workout of choice.

- Slow down! You're likely to ignore this advice if you generally learn quickly. Of course, if you're a quick learner because you already slow down, try slowing down even more. There is a scientific basis behind the saying, "Perfect practice makes perfect." When learning a new skill, you need to keep repeating a precise pattern. The repetition of a pattern creates a neural pathway. Use it enough and it creates a permanent rut. If your pattern is only sort-of-close to what you really want, the new habit will also be just sort-of-close. If you flit around between a few actions that are pretty close, no one pathway will get very robust, and it will be easy to fall back into the old way or slop around between almost-good options.

- How slow? It's hard to be too slow. Think crawl rather than walk. Once you've slowly inched along and gotten a basic grasp of the skill, pay attention and try to hit the sweet spot where you succeed with about eighty percent of your tries and fail only twenty percent or so. That gives you lots of trips down the new pathway and allows for some stretch work to develop additional speed.

- Practice very small steps to almost perfection before you try putting them together in sequence. The temptation will be to move too fast, to try more complex sets of actions. Slow down and perfect the small steps, then master a small sequence of a few steps before you try a complete, complex move.

- Learn your basic moves thoroughly before you try them in a scrimmage—a practice situation that involves many of the complexities of a real situation. Many people have the misunderstanding that trying a new action in a situation that mimics the way you'll eventually use it in the "real" world is a superior way to learn. But learning a move absolutely cold before you add the complexity of multiple moves or environmental obstacles is faster. The practice creates more stability when you finally introduce it into a real situation. Practice in front of the mirror or a video camera, practice in the car by talking to yourself, etc.

- Practice means repeating. In our world, where patience is a dying attribute, practice is a dying art. It's hard to imagine a circumstance where you can repeat something too often. Repetition locks in the learning. Repeating builds neural stability. If you want one secret to successful learning or change, it's repetition. Practice is repetition and repetition is practice.

- When you have a good grasp on a new action, when it becomes a solid habit that occurs with no thought, you need to keep practicing. Slowly raising the quality to an even higher level. Practicing something you're good at, until you're better, is what expertise is all about.

- The art of practice is a balance of how you use your time. The things you're good at need to be practiced to gain maximum benefit from them. Things you're inexperienced at need practice to create diversity and resilience in your game. Things you're not good at need practice to create possibilities that give you options—sometimes unpredictable options are a winning approach. If you practice things you're not that good at, you'll tend to move past the crowd who like the feeling of repeating things they feel good at. If you slow down and precisely practice the small details of things you're already good at, you'll develop quality where others have only comfort. If you practice uncommon actions, you'll boost your game to a level that few casual players will meet.

- If you repeat an old action you've been trying to replace—extinguish—particularly if you tend to fall back into the old action in a pressured situation, set aside time to repeat and repeat the correct action until you can do it even more easily and without thought.

If you participate in a sport or a practice like music or yoga, you can probably see the value of these ideas. But if you didn't read them with a view to professional and business situations, go back and review them. Keep in mind trying to say the right thing in difficult situations or leading meetings where ideas are coming fast and furious. Also think about following through on organizational or project management systems or any of a number of other areas where you want to create change. Many new, non-physical habits can be enhanced by applying the rules.

Go slow, practice small steps, practice when you're good, practice in order to develop new options.

Section 21: **Changing Others**

We all have aspects of our behavior or personalities we'd like to change, but most of us also feel a constant and significant pull to change other people. A pull that usually is greater than the pull to change ourselves. This book is not written to explore that pull in any depth, but a few thoughts about adjusting others' behaviors are worth considering.

If you've taken steps to change your habits, you have a toolbox full of ideas you can transpose into actions to encourage others to change. You can directly explain and encourage or you can begin your mission under the other person's radar.

It's Possible to Change People Without Their Buy In

We are all susceptible to changing our behavior due to outside influences. If we're told we're seriously ill, we may finally start to eat better and exercise. When a product or service line falls below revenue expectations, we may change our way of doing business or drop a product line altogether.

Outside influences work whether they're the circumstances of the market environment—we buy a more fuel-efficient fleet because gas prices go up—or they're purposefully planned and implemented by a person or group—advertising campaigns, political rhetoric or cult recruitment.

Cults and others can certainly use influence badly. There is a whole field of practice that addresses people under undue or destructive influence—influence which does not serve the best interests of the individual it is being used on. I encourage you to learn a bit about this insidious and universal phenomenon as we are all susceptible to being controlled and there are some very clear and practical things you can do to protect yourself, your employees and your loved ones.

Steve Hassan, an expert in the field, has written *Freedom of Mind: Helping Loved Ones Leave Controlling People, Cults and Beliefs*. The information and concepts he details are a solid foundation for becoming aware of undue influences that can enter your life or work environment.

The line between ethical and unethical influence is clear—if you're using influence techniques to help a person broaden their viewpoint, enhance their independence, regulate damaging emotions or achieve goals they have articulated as important, you are clearly being ethical.

You Can Change Your Supervisor or Partner

Nobody likes to feel pressure to change from someone else. This is especially true if you're thinking about changing someone who has equal or more power than you. Plan thoughtfully and proceed very deliberately.

Sometimes when you want someone to change, the situation permits you to say, "I'd like to make this work more smoothly for both of us. How about I try a few things and you let me know what works well for you?" An attitude of "I'll do the work" might allow you to operate a bit more openly.

I've often been able to announce exactly what I'm doing, "I'm looking for ways to get these projects before they're last-minute urgent. I'm going to check with you on projects more often and I hope that helps remind you to give me what you have." Each time it works, I try to acknowledge it in a way that might matter to the person. "I had time to double check that report. That slide deck changed a few times because I had time to run through it numerous times."

Rewards and Acknowledgements

People will tend to repeat behaviors that bring them positive results and rewards.

- If you smile at a person each time they look at you, they will tend to look at you. I use this technique to get a person to focus on me when they're talking to a group. And conversely I look down or look away to encourage a person to address someone other than me.
- If you say "Thank You" when people give you tough feedback, they'll tend to continue the risky behavior of challenging your assumptions.
- If you acknowledge a project or task completed on time, the positive attention will tend to nudge the employee toward getting the next one done on time.
- If you say a cheerful "Good Morning"—without sarcasm—when a chronically tardy employee shows up on time, you're more likely to see a bit more of the same.
- You might also complete a project early when it's handed out early and hold it back until the last minute when it's given to you late. This is different than the traditional "passive-aggressive" attitude in that you're working toward a solution that will help both of you. You just need to be very clear that the goal is a smoother working relationship, not just one that satisfies you— or punishes the other person.

Positive feedback, smiles and noticing other's constructive behaviors all increase the odds of a repeat performance.

Arrange Office Systems and Equipment

Look back at the ideas on arranging the environment to increase your habitual use of systems or decrease your unconscious slips into negative behaviors. Approaches that improve the odds you'll remember your keys and phone and not eat as many snacks, can also help your employees— without them even knowing what's happening.

But it's worth noting, I'm always pleasantly surprised that telling people your strategy can make the results even better—no need to hide your technique.

Patience for the Small Steps

Change is a slow process. Don't try to push an idea too hard. The results are likely to be no better than trying to push a river or a cooked spaghetti noodle—you won't get very far. The better idea is to lead others from a half step in front and look for tiny changes.

Demonstrate the small steps you are working on. Humbly expose your setbacks and efforts to change. Quietly share a minor success to highlight the value of the process instead of emphasizing only the realization of the large goal. And confess your slipups to raise awareness and make acknowledging mistakes more acceptable.

Don't Let Success Raise Your Expectations Too Quickly

There is an odd behavior many of us get into. When a person finally starts to change, we seem to naturally raise our expectations that they will accelerate the process and change all the things that bother us. We fall into pointing out the other behaviors we want adjusted or how much further they need to go to completely change their old habits.

Remind yourself to quietly persist not push. This particular project will be brought to fruition by being a doggedly determined strategist. Like an ancient hunter, don't try to run them down. Just patiently and strategically walk their obstructive behavior to death.

Use Negatives Judiciously

Positive reactions are almost always the most powerful change agents. Occasionally you need to make them even more notable. One approach is to very carefully mix in a few negatives. The difference or texture between positive and negative can make the positives feel more positive. Think of your delight in a warm sunny day after a run of rainy or wintery weather.

Getting an effective mix of positive reactions and negative feedback is very tricky since we humans are programed to notice negative things—threatening things. Studies suggest that a mix of three or four positive to one negative is a reasonable goal. The trouble is that most of us don't recognize the multiple times we respond with a discouraging or negative response.

If the person you're trying to influence does the thing you're trying to discourage you can react with a negative, but avoid being so negative or critical that you knock their socks off. You're trying to encourage a step toward a positive behavior not arouse defensiveness.

Mild negative reactions you might try:
- Look away.
- Freeze and let the quiet become uncomfortable.
- Keep a neutral facial expression.
- Delay responding—this can work particularly well when the person is inappropriately trying to get your attention during your private time.

Be aware that it is hard to modulate negative approaches—nagging, blaming, critiquing, threatening, intimidating tone or body language and many other variations that we tend to use in our attempts to convince someone to change. You'll need to change first before you're effective at changing the other person.

Strategize the Next Steps

If you have a plan, it's easier to stay on track. There is something about knowing the next step that helps many people relax and work on the present. The continuity between the current small step and the stairway to the final goal corrals an urge to push too far too fast.

An example might be helpful:

- When you wish your boss would be more respectful, the first step might be to stop looking down or away and simply meet his eyes during his outbursts. Erode the idea you will just take what's dished out.

  The next step might be to ask, during a quiet time, how you can help set things up so that problems can be solved with less stress on both of you. Your question acknowledges the issue without directly confronting.

  After you've had a few conversations you might be ready to say during an outburst, "I'm having trouble following what you're saying. I want to be able to improve—or solve this issue." Avoid casting blame, you don't want to encourage defensiveness.

  You hope that eventually you have the safety to say, "When you get this intense I have trouble thinking well, I'm going to need to take a quick break to use the bathroom. And then I'd like to start again and move this forward."

Changing other people takes as much exploration of possible approaches as does changing yourself. The point is to strategize then implement and evaluate until you have enough additional information to be certain your approach is working.

Conclusion

If you want a specific outcome, change needs to be deliberate. If you wait passively for change to happen, or expect it to happen serendipitously, you'll get whatever card is on top of the deck.

Change can sometimes be almost effortless, if you're willing to slow down and plan it out. You now have some valuable tools to try anytime you need them.

My top hints? I'd have to put repetition at the head of the list. Repetition is how we build habits. Repetition is a simple concept to understand. There is no skill involved in repeating something an additional time. Take a minute, decide what to practice and slowly do it again and again.

- Pick up your floss. Put it down. Pick it up again. You're more likely to use it next time you get ready for bed.
- Do the same with the question you want to lead with when you assign a project to an employee. "Do you have what you need to complete the project on time at the most effective cost?" Now repeat it again.
- Create a task list today. Update your task list tomorrow. Review it and update it the next day.
- Set your alarm and get up. Repeat the next morning.
- Stop when you feel irritation. Think, *Breathe before you say anything*. Say it again.

It's also important to have a clear idea of what you're heading toward—your goals or the outcomes you want. Try to find things that are important to you and their value to you will tend to pull you forward. Goals focus your efforts and attention. They keep you pointed at a vision of a better future. They also keep you from getting distracted by a short-term feeling or bright-shiny object.

If you have a goal, then getting there is a series of small steps or next actions. You don't need to—and in fact can't—do more than that. Simply take the next step. You're one step closer. And each step will make it easier to take the next one—step, repeat, step, repeat.

Each time you try something new, if you're paying attention, you'll learn something. So take a step, learn something, adjust. Take a step, learn something, adjust. That's the process of change at its most fundamental.

It's hard to get past resistance and inertia to try what we would like to change. You're capable of change, but discouragement can get in the way. Why keep trying if you've failed before? I think Wayne Gretzky the hockey player summed it up best, "You miss 100% of the shots you don't take." So take a shot!

Hire a Coach

You can change all by yourself. But I encourage you to take some advice from the world's top professional and amateur athletes, and musicians. Pay attention to the CEOs of many Fortune 500 companies and to performers. Consider hiring a coach. A coach gives you access to an alternative viewpoint that can expand your thinking and help you see things that are in your blind spot.

The more times a person goes through the process of strategizing an approach to making changes, the more information and experience they have. A good coach has been there many times, has seen the difficulties, has seen how to get results and has a wealth of information and experience.

Again and again, managing partners, CEOs and entrepreneurs tell me they're astonished at how helpful it is to work with a coach. Many of them say that they feel what they've learned from our sessions and their practice has helped them bring their teams and businesses to new levels. It's also worth noting that many individuals I've coached say that they took home skills and attitudes they learned and that benefited their families.

For a lot of self-made individuals, coaching is a new experience—a change. I encourage you to give it a try and see what you learn. Then apply what you've learned, adjust and take another step.

Acknowledgments

From First Edition

I coach because I like to learn. My clients have always been a rich source of both challenges and solutions. The people who've invited me to guide them through a rough patch or help them build a more satisfying future gave me the priceless gift of their trust and the chance to try out new ideas and tools. Most of what I know about change I owe to them.

I tend to like my own writing. And then someone tells me they don't understand what I'm trying to say and I reread what I thought was wonderful prose. At that moment I often realize I also can't figure out what I was trying to say. Critical readers and editors are necessary to those of us who read for understanding and insight.

Many people helped me take my drafts and turn them into a more coherent form. Early on my wife Szifra read what I had compiled and encouraged me to keep working with numerous ideas and questions. The much improved draft then started its journey and got all sorts of additional tweaking from Lisa Hochstein, Anne Jolles, Robin Dowling, Perry Woodward, Anna Huckabee-Tull, Hope Gulker, Joni Lippa and Ron Cooper.

Sarah Reiff-Hekking, my coaching colleague and Thursday morning writing partner added ideas about content and helped further shape the prose. When I ran dry of ideas or motivation, her steady encouragement to not get bogged down was like a splash of cool water. Coaching, even peer coaching, is a truly amazing process when you sit across from someone like Sarah who strives for quality and always delivers respect.

When I thought it might help clarify what I was suggesting, sections went out to my clients and they were kind enough to appreciate the content and not point out the ugly scars that still needed polishing. They found ways to turn those early concepts into tools they could use to grow and change their behavior.

There comes a time in a manuscript's life when it demands the eye of an experienced editor. If the author has my thin skin, the editor needs to have a thoughtful style while pruning back the overgrowth. JoSelle Vanderhooft found the right touch to challenge me while supporting my voice. She poured hundreds of comments into the ground where I had planted a few flowers and she helped create a garden that felt like it still belonged to me.

To move a manuscript to a form that makes it available to a wider audience takes a project manager who can negotiate the complex possibilities of the new digital and print media services. My wife Szifra Birke tackles involved projects with her coaching clients and invested that same level of commitment in this project. I wouldn't be who I am and this book wouldn't be what it is without her.

Second edition acknowledgements

After extensive rewrites, my wife Szifra Birke dug in and once again, smoothed out the rough spots. She pushed me to shorten, simplify and clarify. She also keeps encouraging me to write and points out sections she says are "great!" And she laughs at my jokes. All any writer could ask. Thank you Szifra!

Author's Biography

Jay's professional practice focused on building the most positive, satisfying and productive relationships with partners, team members and clients. He was a go-to consultant for teams that found themselves tangled up in negative interactions.

Jay enjoys being an interpreter at the intersection of research, philosophy and simple practical solutions. His wealth of information and engaging questions have a knack for opening up conversations that are begging to be explored.

Jay brings a renaissance background to his consulting and life. His career path has included experience as a therapist, fundraiser, dog behaviorist, graduate level academic evaluator, news photographer, certified Master Mechanic, prize winning boat builder, licensed sailboat delivery captain, finish carpenter and pioneer in Emergency Medical Response.

He has an MA in counseling psychology. That understanding of individuals' emotional and cognitive processes is integrated with his experience working in business and professional practices. His extensive knowledge of organizational systems and scenario planning adds a viewpoint that is highly valued. He has also been lauded for his employee training and retention practices.

Jay has coached and consulted with for-profit and non-profit organizations and high-powered individuals for over thirty five years. His clients have included auto manufacturers, service companies, professional practices, small manufacturers, government-regulated firms, healthcare organizations and performing artists as well as nationally recognized names in the fields of financial investing, professional sports, entertainment corporations and publishing. He currently invests his time and energy in helping new managers in the non-profit space, and writing books, articles and blogs.

His consulting has brought value to businesses ranging from single entrepreneurs to multimillion-dollar corporations. In the 1970's an adult educational project Jay designed and implemented was praised by Ralph Nader as one of the best in the country. His media appearances include PBS's NOVA.

Jay is an active Laser sailboat racer, an endurance bicyclist and a light-weight backpacker. He blogs at PracticeSimpleSteps.com. He lives in Lowell, Massachusetts with his tolerant wife, Szifra Birke, and his boisterous Airedale Gus.

Bibliography

Amabile, Teresa, and Steve Kramer. *The Progress Principle: Using Small Wins to Ignite Joy, Engagement and Creativity at Work.* Boston: Harvard Business Review Press, 2011.

Baumeister, Roy F., and John Tierney. *Willpower: Rediscovering the Greatest Human Strength.* London: Penguin Books, 2011.

Brian Wansink, PhD. *Mindless Eating: Why We Eat More Than We Think.* Bantum Books, 2006.

Coyle, Daniel. *The Little Book of Talent: 52 Tips for Improving Your Skills.* New York: Random House, 2012.

Deitch, Joseph. *Elvate: An Essential Guide to Life.* Greenleaf Book Group Press, 2018.

Duhigg, Charles. *The Power of Habit: Why We Do What We Do in Life and Business.* New York: Random House, 2012.

Hassan, Steve. *Freedom of Mind: Helping Loved Ones Leave Controlling People, Cults and Beliefs.* Newton, MA: Freedom of Mind Press, 2013.

Heath, Chip, and Dan Heath. *Switch: How to Change Things When Change is Hard.* Crown Business, 2010.

Kahneman, Daniel. *Thinking, Fast and Slow.* New York: Farrah, Straus and Giroux, 2011.

Kegan, Robert, and Lisa Laskow Lahey. *Immunity to Change: How to Overcome it and Unlock the Potential in Yourself and Your Organization.* Boston: Harvard Business Press, 2009.

Lemov, Doug, Erica Woolway, and Katie Yezzi. *Practice Perfect: 42 Rules for Getting Better at Getting Better.* San Francisco: Jossey-Bass, 2012.

Norcross, John C., and Kristin Loberg. *Changeology.* Simon and Schuster, 2012.

Pink, Daniel H. *Drive: The Surprising Truth About What Motivates Us.* Riverhead Hardcover, 2009.

Schulz, Kathryn. *Being Wrong: Adventures in the Margin of Error.* Ecco, 2010.

Scott, Susan. *Fierce Conversations: Achieving Sucess at Work.* Penguin Group/Viking Studio, 2002.